A Mission To Millions

The Amazing Story Of Ernie Allen And The Every Home Crusade

BY

Victor Maxwell

Belfast Northern Ireland **Greenville** South Carolina

A MISSION TO MILLIONS

ISBN 1 84030 069 8

Ambassador Publications
a division of
Ambassador Productions Ltd.
Providence House
16 Hillview Avenue,
Belfast, BT5 6JR
Northern Ireland

Emerald House
1 Chick Springs Road, Suite 203
Greenville,
South Carolina 29609, USA
www.emeraldhouse.com

FOREWORD

I was a teenager and a new convert when I first met Ernie Allen. As a young postman I delivered international mail almost every day to his home at 95 Omeath Street. In conversation with him he introduced me to his soul stirring revival publications and the names of such great preachers as Charles G. Finney and Rueben A. Torrey. I not only sensed that this was a godly man, but I was impressed that he had a deep passion for a practical revival - not the sort of revival that is often measured by having more good meetings, but a genuine revival that results in the salvation of the lost. Besides having this vision and burden, Ernie Allen also fired the souls of other Christians to become involved.

Through our early encounter with Ernie we were invited to help in some of the great gospel crusades he organised in Belfast. When he ventured into the work of the Every Home Crusade I was again challenged by his zeal and soon got involved in placing gospel literature in every home in Dunmurry, near Belfast.

Ernie's vision and passion to win lost people for Jesus Christ soon widened to embrace multitudes of people beyond the shores of the British Isles. Like Joseph, of whom his father Jacob prophesied, "Joseph is a fruitful bough, even a fruitful bough by a well; whose branches run over the wall," Ernie's fruitful ministry has crossed over the walls of cultural and linguistic frontiers to bring in a great harvest of souls all around the world.

Years after our early involvement with the Every Home Crusade, my wife and I served as missionaries with Acre Gospel Mission and travelled on the upper tributaries of Brazil's great Amazon River, taking Christ's gospel to the isolated population in the forest. On those journeys we distributed Every Home Crusade scripture booklets, leaflets and posters which were sent from Belfast.

During our last few years in Brazil the basement of our home was a distribution depot for the Every Home Crusade Scripture booklets and gospel tracts in Portuguese. From the basement depot the paper missionaries were distributed all over the Amazon and Acre by pastors and colporteurs.

Being privileged to be acquainted with this work from its early beginnings and then to witness its effect in distant lands has made us aware of how strategic and effective this ministry is. However, it takes more than paper to do God's work. God uses people. You can never estimate the value and impact of one life that is wholly given to the Lord. Ernie Allen has been God's man whose vision and steps of faith not only challenged many young Christians like myself, but through his obedience to Jesus Christ, the Lord has made him a blessing to millions.

As I contemplated the conclusion of this book Annie Booth-Clibborn's hymn seemed to sum up the life of Ernie Allen and the work of the Every Home Crusade.

There is no gain but by a loss,
We cannot save but by the Cross;
The corn of wheat to multiply,

Must fall into the ground and die.
Oh, should a soul alone remain
When it a hundredfold can gain?

Our souls are held by all they hold;
Slaves still are slaves in chains of gold.
To whatsoever we may cling,
We make it a soul-chaining thing,
Whether it be a life or land,
And dear as our right eye or hand.

Whenever you ripe fields behold,
Waving to God their sheaves of gold,
Be sure some corn of wheat has died,
Some saintly soul been crucified:
Someone has suffered, wept and prayed,
And fought hell's legions undismayed!

This book tells only part of the story. The whole story will be fully revealed in eternity.

Victor Maxwell

Contents

Chapter One

Here, There and Every Home

If busyness is the cheapest form of medicine, then the place that I tell you of must be a tonic. The factory is a large two story brick building providing fourteen thousand square feet of floor space and is neatly tucked behind a terrace of houses and shops on Belfast's Castlereagh Road. The forecourt opens onto Clara Street and provides parking for a dozen cars. Today there are no cars in the forecourt. Instead, a truck laden with an eighteen tonne load dominates the parking zone. The container it carries is bound for the Indian city of Madras and is full of millions of colourful booklets and leaflets in eleven Indian languages. One container load is sent to Madras every month.

In another area a fork-lift shuttles between the factory and another container as large as the one headed to India. The plastic covered stacks of colourful leaflets and booklets are carefully placed in the metal container until it is full. The shipment will be opened again only when it arrives in Nigeria where the precious contents will be distributed throughout the country. When this load is transported from the loading bay, another eighteen tonnes of Spanish literature are due to be dispatched for Venezuela. Yet another eighteen tonnes of John's Gospel in the English language are ready for shipment to Ghana in West Africa, and consignments of similar tonnage are being prepared for Kenya, Brazil and the Philippines. The cost of the paper, printing and shipping of an eighteen tonne container of literature is approximately £25,000.

Inside the gateway cubed stacks of white paper rise high on either side like mini-sky scrapers. They form a narrow corridor which leads to the factory floor. Here nineteen men ply their skills attending to their jobs. The whirr, buzz and hiss of eleven large Heildelberg printing machines and Sthal folders operating simultaneously is deafening. Those attending the machines wear large ear muffs which make them look more like aircraft controllers.

From one machine alone 8,000 sheets of colourful type are printed every hour, and each sheet makes two booklets. Simple mathematics verify that one machine can produce over 100,000 booklets per day. The factory uses sixty tonnes of paper every month at a cost of £30,000.

Added to all this there are other presses which also run constantly, printing different booklets in various languages and in full colour. It is not surprising to learn that in the factory three tonnes of paper are used up every day. During the last year over 44,000,000 publications, in seventy different languages, were sent to over one hundred countries from this remarkable factory.

Other machines fold, cut and staple while two young men fill wooden tea chests or cardboard boxes with the valuable publications. The finished product is then lifted by a trolley or fork-lift to a storeroom in another part of the city. In another room two men wrap smaller quantities of literature in scores of parcels to be sent to addresses all over the world. These are collected every day by a red Parcel Force truck and transported to the post office for distribution.

Situated at the front of the building is a suite of offices, each one responsible for the different departments of this factory.

The accounts office is especially important for this non-profit organisation as it took £884,818 to cover production costs in 1998. The design and production office is the nerve centre of this operation. One long shelf is totally occupied with Bibles in many languages. Projects and letters pile high on one desk, and computers fill another. Across the corridor are two other offices, and here the many letters that pour into this factory are processed daily.

In one of the rooms above the factory offices all the workers meet at the beginning of each day for a devotional reading and a time of prayer to ask God's blessing and favour on all their work. Another second floor room is a sorting department from where literature is dispatched to seeking souls and young converts.

This factory is the headquarters of The Every Home Crusade.

To these headquarters reports filter back from all over the world to the smallest office in the building. The door is closed and an elderly man prayerfully mulls over and deals with the correspondence which arrives each day. The colourful stamps from all over the world would make the office a dream come true for any philatelist. The simple hand writing on each envelope indicates that for many who write, English is not their first language. One by one the letters are opened. They come from pastors, evangelists, missionaries, teachers, prisoners, nurses and doctors. Many letters report the latest news of those who are engaged in the distribution of the literature and give thrilling accounts of conversions to Jesus Christ in distant lands. Much of the correspondence that arrives is from inquirers who have read the literature, and they either send the news of their conversion to Jesus Christ or want to ask more questions about the way of salvation.

Other letters request large numbers of booklets and tracts to use in particular languages, and sometimes requests are made with upcoming gospel crusades in mind. Demand and supply are a vital stimulus in the growth of this ministry, and they are ever stretching the Crusade to greater and better limits of production.

Still other envelopes contain the needed gifts from donors who faithfully support this work because they have confidence in the power of the gospel on the printed page to win many souls to the Lord Jesus Christ. The Every Home Crusade send literature free of charge to numerous countries in order to fulfil the command of our Lord Jesus Christ to preach and publish the gospel to every creature. The amount of correspondence that arrives shows that this ministry is reaching people from every land.

• • •

For twenty years Miss Maizie Smyth has been a missionary with Unevangelised Field Missions Worldwide in the Democratic Republic of the Congo. During much of that time she has also been associated with the Every Home Crusade outreach. As she served the Lord in the Congo her heart was burdened for all Africans of many nations. As a result of her forced absence from the Congo due to civil war, Maizie was able to become involved in the work in other parts of the African continent.

She spent a period in Gabon, West Africa, and she shared with Christian leaders there the effective use of the Every Home Crusade literature which she had obtained in French to use among the people in the Congo. She wrote from Gabon:

> During my visit I had the opportunity of visiting about twenty different churches and evangelistic organisations who are working in Gabon. It was disappointing to realise that in the shopping areas of Gabon's major cities there are no Christian bookshops. This means that people have difficulty obtaining Christian reading material. There is one Christian book shop in the suburbs of Libreville which supplies fifty colporteurs with books and material to maintain book tables in many rural villages.
>
> The leaders of one church requested 20,000 Gospels of John, 20,000 copies of "The Way of Salvation", 20,000

copies of "The Gospel of Jesus Christ" and 20,000 copies of "Pardon and Assurance" booklets. Different departments of the Christian and Missionary Alliance Church also requested a total of 35,000 of the four booklets which we print in the French language.

At the Christian hospital in Bolongola all members of the medical staff are required to follow the "One-to-one Evangelism Course" and are now nurse/evangelists at the hospital. This has resulted in over six thousand people professing faith in Christ over this past year. "If only we had literature to give to these new believers," was the plea of the chaplain. He has requested 5,000 copies of each of the four booklets which we print in French.

Three Christian organisations work into the neighbouring country of Equatorial Guinea with its population of half a million people. These friends requested 27,000 booklets in Spanish for their work. There is also an outreach team working into Sao Tome, an island of 132,000 Portuguese speaking inhabitants. They have requested 16,000 booklets in the Portuguese language.

In response to Maizie's letter Every Home Crusade made plans to ship an eighteen tonne container full of French Gospels of John and other Scripture booklets to Gabon.

• • •

Madras, India - just the name of the place conjures up a picture of teeming masses of people, crowded trains, busy streets, blasting horns, rickshaws and bicycles. Markets are busy. Sari clad ladies and men dressed in white suits with coloured turbans trade their wares. The smell of a thousand spices fills the air. This multilingual country has manifold religions, and superstition is rife.

This is the land that gave us tea and curry. It was also to this land that the first missionaries of the Modern Missionary

Movement went over two hundred years ago. Last year the Every Home Crusade sent more than two hundred tonnes of literature to the India Bible Literature Mission in Madras. From there it was delivered to evangelists and churches in strategic centres all over India.

Years have proved that this is a rewarding investment. Letters have returned from the Indian sub-continent recounting great blessings wherever the printed page travels. Tens of thousands of people have been converted, and thousands of new Christian groups have been formed through the Lord's blessing on these printed leaflets.

• • •

The Municipal Market is one of the busiest places in Manaus, Brazil. It is a place where locals come early every day to buy their fresh vegetables, fruit, meat and fish. Thousands of other people use the sprawling single story complex as a thoroughfare on their way from the nearby port to the city centre. The foul odour of decaying meat and innards of fish mingle with the wafting aroma of garlic and aniseed and the added sweet smell of tropical fruits.

Undoubtedly the busiest place in the market is the main entrance where the hustle and bustle of dealers and traders compete with the chatter and calls of passers-by greeting each other or catching up on the latest gossip. Stepping out of the bright sunlight into the shadow just beyond the large open gate, no one can miss noticing two large posters on the wall between two kiosks. Both posters give the essence of the gospel message: "Jesus said, 'I am the Way the Truth and the Life. No man cometh unto the Father but by Me.'" "For there is one God, and one Mediator between God and man, the Man Christ Jesus who gave His life a ransom for many..." These posters were published and sent to Brazil by the Every Home Crusade.

For many years, Hazel Miskimmin, a missionary with the Acre Gospel Mission, went daily to the market place and took her post at a small wooden booth where she had an ample supply of Every Home Crusade gospel booklets in Portuguese, English and Spanish. It was not necessary for her to distribute the literature because people, young and old and from all walks of life, frequently stopped at the booth to ask for the booklets and engage in conversation about spiritual matters.

Over a period of four years of being involved in this ministry Hazel saw more than three hundred people put their trust in Jesus Christ. Many of the converts came from notorious backgrounds of crime and immorality. One young man, Mario, was desperate to get right with God. He unashamedly knelt on the ground at the entrance to the market and accepted Jesus Christ as Saviour. As a result of his conversion, all the members of his family have now become Christians, and one of his brothers is involved in Christian work as a pastor in Acre, Brazil.

• • •

Francisco pulled his crude canoe alongside the wooden boardwalk of a small riverside town on a tributary of the Amazon River. Many Christians gathered round to welcome and greet their friend Francisco. His broad grin revealed his obvious satisfaction in seeing his friends, and after some animated greetings he pulled back the protecting tarpaulin that covered the canoe's cargo to reveal eight large tea chests dominating the centre of the canoe. In a country famous for its coffee one would not think that the arrival of tea from India would be hailed with such enthusiasm nor would there be a lucrative market for this beverage, at least not in such quantities. One by one the heavy tea chests were placed on the shoulders of volunteer carriers who transported them to the back room of a little Assembly of God Church. No time was wasted in opening the chests with some strong leverage on a crowbar. Under the lid, thick black plastic covered the contents, and when this was cut open there were shouts of "Amen" and "Alleluia" which rang round the small room. Bronzed hands delved into the open boxes and lifted out the precious contents, not tea, but colourful booklets bearing the title "O Caminho da Salvacao": "The Way of Salvation". The other boxes contained tens of thousands of gospel tracts in the Portuguese language.

Francisco was not a river merchant plying his wares. He was a colporteur who travelled extensively on the Amazon water ways sowing the good seed of God's Word. He received the literature from the Every Home Crusade via another missionary from Northern Ireland, Fred Orr. Fred has many workers who distribute tonnes of literature to churches and colporteurs throughout the needy region.

• • •

One Sunday evening Harold Mawhinney in Banbridge Baptist Church enthusiastically sang,

"O happy day that fixed my choice
On Thee my Saviour and My God."

That happy day of his conversion is traced back to a gospel tract that was slipped through the door of his father's house in the village of Gilford. Noel Turkington, John Dickson and a party of friends conducted open-air meetings in the townlands and villages from Banbridge to Gilford and placed Every Home Crusade literature in every home. As a result of reading R. A. Torrey's booklet, "The Way of Salvation Made Plain", William Mawhinney, the father of eight boys and two daughters, put his trust in the Saviour. Watson, his oldest son, also read the tract and followed his father in seeking the Saviour as did his wife. Father and son prayed for the rest of the family, and God's blessing came upon that home. Over a short period of time seven of the Mawhinney brothers were converted.

The Mawhinney brothers were gifted and endowed with musical talents, and they travelled all over Northern Ireland singing, testifying and preaching the gospel of the Lord Jesus Christ. Through their witness others came to the Saviour too.

The leaflet, "Safety Certainty and Enjoyment", was instrumental in bringing about the conversion of Harold's mother-in-law. All of this work was accomplished through the initial seed sown when one piece of Every Home Crusade literature was placed through a letter box.

• • •

Las Muelles de Cariaco is the name of mountains that skirt around Caracas, the capital of Venezuela. Just a few years ago a severe earthquake shook the whole area and caused much havoc. Several evangelical churches in the hills suffered severe structural damage, and this caused the churches in the capital to reach out to help them.

Pastor Engles, a Dutch missionary, related his experience when he visited one of these damaged churches.

> While we talked to the pastor about the free evangelistic literature we had in the van, some Christians present began to cry and said, "Praise the Lord! We thought that God had forgotten us." The literature has been a great blessing and encouragement to these people.
>
> In the small village of El Baul an old man asked his grandson to read every evening a portion of a booklet, "The Pardon For Sin". One chapter in the booklet explains why Christians are a happy people. Grandmother, who also attended the evening readings said that she still did not understand why Christians were so happy and she wanted to know more. They decided to invite a Christian brother to explain these things to them. After hearing the explanation grandmother accepted Jesus Christ as Saviour.
>
> At Acariga I had to go through a vehicle check point which was manned by soldiers of the National Guard. One of these men in uniform wanted to know what I was carrying in the boxes in the back of the car. I showed him the "Seven

Steps to Knowing God in the Gospel of John" and "The Pardon for Sin" and took the opportunity to preach the gospel to him. He was visibly touched, and before I left I had the privilege of pointing him to Jesus Christ. He asked me what he had to do after his conversion. I told him to look out for an evangelical church and attend there.

Some months later I had to pass another National Guard check point. Suddenly, out of the darkness some one shouted, "Hermano, don't you remember me?" It was the same soldier I had prayed with at Acariga. He had joined a good church and had already been baptised.

The literature you sent us has been distributed amongst the churches, especially the small and poorer churches in the interior. We estimate that some 1,800 churches have received the literature, and it is impossible to describe the blessing and the exact numbers of people who have been saved. Last year, after we received the container of Spanish publications, we backed a summer evangelistic crusade with door to door witnessing using your literature. At least 400 people trusted Christ as Saviour, and up until today they are attending local churches.

• • •

Hector, like many other Filipinos, left his native country to find work in other parts of the world ostensibly to send money back home to his family in Manila. However, his hard earned money was often squandered on unrestrained binges of alcohol and drugs. Finally, broken in body, Hector returned to Manila where he was interned in hospital and diagnosed as having cirrhosis of the liver.

Christians from the "Sowers of the Light Ministries" who heard of his plight visited Hector in hospital and read to him from the Gospel of John in his native Tagalog language. Even though he was seriously ill he listened attentively to the "Seven Steps to Knowing God". When the friends had finished reading the leaflet Hector repeated the sinner's prayer and signed his name at the front of the booklet. He showed real evidence of being born again and faced death with the assurance that he was going to be with Christ.

At his funeral some weeks later fifteen of his relatives and friends were also led to faith in Jesus Christ.

• • •

Pixie Caldwell has been a missionary for many years with Action Partners in Nigeria, West Africa's largest republic. During some of this time she worked with the Fulani people of whom there are 25,000,000. Not only are most of the Fulani people Moslem, but they are considered to be one of the least evangelised tribes in Africa and are scattered over sixteen countries.

On one occasion while based in a Fulani village, Pixie arranged that a friend pick her up and take her to a meeting. Alas, that person got lost and did not arrive at the prearranged time. As the sun quickly sank towards the horizon and dusk drew on, Pixie was welcomed by some ladies into a small round mud hut while she waited for her delayed friend.

By the dim light of a bush lamp, Pixie sat chatting with the Fulani women who readily shared their maize porridge with their missionary guest. As Pixie talked with the ladies she produced some gospel tracts and booklets and began to share their contents with the ladies. Very soon many outstretched hands reached through the low doorway. It was the men wanting a copy of the Scripture booklets and tracts. Custom dictated that Muslim men could not enter a women's hut, but it did not stop them hearing the Good News.

Later that night, as was her habit at the end of each day, Pixie prayed God's blessing upon His Word that had been shared.

Two years later, a Fulani man arrived at the house were Pixie was staying. His face was radiant as he announced, "Through the literature you gave me I believed the gospel, but I haven't seen you before!"

Pixie pondered what he had said. *How could I have given him a tract and yet have never seen him?*

Then she remembered that this man must have received the literature the night she had been delayed. She vividly recollected that although she could not see their faces their hands reached through the door way for the Christian literature.

By the power of the gospel told on the printed page the Fulani man, Abe, was converted. He had taken the tract with him to the government office where he worked, and during some free time he read about the Saviour. As he read the few pages a pastor noticed and asked if he understood what he was reading. That pastor not only helped Abe call upon God for salvation but became a great help to Abe after his conversion. It is not easy for this new convert. Like other converted Moslems Abe has suffered persecution because of the confession of his faith in Jesus Christ. His house was even burned down by fanatical Moslems. He needs the Lord's protection.

• • •

Mr. Stephen and his friends distributed tracts every Saturday morning on the busy streets of Bristol, England. He wrote, "On Sunday night we met a young man at our church who came to know the Lord through one of your tracts. He received it on Saturday and had taken it home. He tore the tract up but said something told him he must read it. He pieced the leaflet together again and read the gospel message. He said, 'I knew when I read it that it was for me.' The great thing about this conversion is that the Word of God in the tract drew the young man. I didn't even get the opportunity to witness to him."

• • •

On board the naval frigate H. M. S. Ajax a naval officer wrote, "I am so glad to report that I am no longer the only Christian on board this ship. The Lord has saved another lad. It is better than a tonic to see the change in him. I am sure the Lord is working in other hearts. The tracts you sent are having the desired effect. Please pray for our witness and send more literature."

• • •

There is no life so lonely as one spent behind prison bars. One young man wrote to the Every Home Crusade from a prison cell in England: "I am writing to thank you for the help I have had from reading your literature which was sent to me by a friend. As you will see from this letter I am in prison, but I may add that I am glad to be here. It is here that I came to know Jesus Christ; I have come to know myself, and I have come to know that I can live without alcohol. I know that with the help of the Lord, I will never drink again. I am sending some support for your work."

• • •

These are only samplings of tens of thousands of reports that have flooded into the Every Home Crusade in response to their printed material that has circulated worldwide during the last fifty years.

When William Caxton published the first English language book in December 1475, there was no way he could have imagined the flood of literature that would develop in its wake. We have come a long way since those early type-setting skills which involved the arduous use of wood-cut symbols. Modern computerised screening has not only replaced the lead characters and type cast plates which were used for hundreds of years, but it has completely revolutionised the printing industry, and the development of new and improved technology is still ongoing.

However, in spite of the growth and change of the printing revolution, there is one thing about this industry that has not changed - the power, importance and impact of the printed page. Printed paper still remains one of the most potent communication tools of our time.

The one who said, "Give me twenty-six lead soldiers and I will change the world", knew the dynamic potential of the printed page. Almost five hundred years ago Martin Luther said, "We must throw the printer's ink bottle at the devil." That is what he did. The great Protestant Reformation was cradled in the printing press. The rapid spread of the Reformation was greatly enhanced by the blessing and benefit of Bibles printed in the language of the people and the circulation of the writings of the great reformers.

Books, newspapers, magazines, leaflets and booklets are more than ever part of our every day lives, and literature continues to make a great impact on our society, for better and for worse. Nigeria, the Philippines, India, Venezuela, Brazil, England and Northern Ireland are only a few of the more than one hundred countries from where reports of the use of literature justify the maxim, "A drop of ink can make a million think."

God is blessing this work in hospitals, prisons, schools, colleges, army barracks, markets and fairs where millions of Every Home Crusade leaflets and booklets are touching millions of people and changing their lives and that in spite of their cultural or ethnic peculiarities.

In the Every Home Crusade office, the reports brought by the letters are shared with the workers. These workers are foreign missionaries, yet they do not travel abroad to preach their message. They send out their "printed missionaries" which are fluent in more than seventy languages to more than one hundred countries on our planet. The letters bring greetings from Christians they have never met. The mail reports conversions to Jesus Christ in distant lands to which they may never travel. They enjoy fellowship with Christian brothers and sisters they do not personally know.

However, no matter what the nature of the letter may be, invariably all the correspondence begins with the same simple phrase, "Dear Mr. Allen..."

Who is Mr. Allen? What is this printing organisation? Let me tell you this amazing story.

Chapter Two

ROOTS AND SHOOTS

In 1903 the American evangelist, Dr. Rueben A. Torrey and his song leader, Dr. Charles Alexander, visited Northern Ireland and conducted a month of evangelistic meetings in Belfast. Their presence made quite a stir in the province as night after night thousands of people attended the services. Dr. Torrey preached soul-stirring messages, and Dr. Alexander led the crowd in singing what he called the "Glory Song."

When all my labours and trials are o'er,
And I am safe on that beautiful shore,
Just to be near the dear Lord I adore,
Will through the ages be glory for me.

Oh, that will be glory for me,
When by His grace, I shall look on His face,
That will be glory, be glory for me.

Dr. Alexander introduced his hymn book, the Alexander Hymn Book No. 3, during these meetings.

The attendance at the services increased weekly posing a problem of where to hold the meetings. Every night hundreds of people responded to the preaching of the renowned evangelist. The number of people grew so large that no church or public meeting hall in Belfast could accommodate the crowds that flocked into the meetings. It was due to this dilemma that the organisers decided to hold the meetings in St. George's Market.

The numbers reached a climax on the final day of the campaign when more than two thousand people attended each of the three open-air meetings. On that evening more than seven thousand people attended the meeting at St. George's Market, and many were not able to gain admittance into the building. Considering there was no electronic equipment to amplify the preacher's voice, it was a great undertaking for the preacher to address such numbers. God greatly blessed his servants. The multitudes sang Alexander's hymns, and when Torrey rose to preach, the power of God fell on the meeting. Over five hundred people professed to trust Jesus Christ as Saviour on that night.

Dr. Torrey's meetings caused a great stirring among mill workers all over Belfast. Hundreds of them were converted at these evangelistic meetings. Martha Girvan was one of these converts. She lived near Duncairn Gardens in North Belfast and worked at the Jennymount Mill. Above the noise of the busy looms she would hear girls' voices throughout the day singing Alexander's "Glory Song," and even while walking to work at six o'clock in the morning some of the mill workers blended their voices and raised a few verses of Alexander's hymns.

The excitement of other girls talking about the meetings encouraged Martha to attend and hear this eloquent and effective evangelist. Not only was she captivated by the inspirational singing, but it seemed that when Torrey rose to preach Martha was overcome with the sense of sin and her need of the Saviour. She called upon the Lord to save her that night, and her life was greatly changed.

Another change occurred in Martha's life when she met a young man called William Allen. He worked at Belfast's Harland and Wolff shipyard which at that time was not only the leading shipyard in the world but was also the largest employer in Belfast. William worked in the shadow of the Olympic and the Titanic, the two most modern vessels of that time. Martha and William were soon going out together and later got married.

Martha brought the atmosphere of the Torrey revival meetings to her home through the hymns she had learned out of the Alexander hymn book. She prayed earnestly for the family that God would give her. The Lord blessed the Allen home with five children: Elizabeth, Maud, Jessie, Ernest and Mabel.

Before Ernest was born William was injured in an accident in the shipyard and as a result had to terminate his employment there. After this he moved with his wife and their young family out of the city to a more rural environment near the Annahilt Presbyterian Church, two miles out of Hillsborough in the beautiful rolling hills of County Down.

Ernest, like his sisters, attended the local elementary school. Little did young Ernest know that when he learned the twenty-six letters of the alphabet they would play a major role in the ministry of printing that God had already planned for him in his future.

Life in the country was great for the Allen girls and their only brother. After school each day Ernest would help round up the cattle and feed the livestock at a local farm. Before the advent of modern machinery, tilling the ground and bringing in the harvest were occasions in which all the family was involved, and Ernest enjoyed it.

Annahilt Presbyterian Church was the centre of life for this farming community, and their principal services were well attended. Most people walked to church although some came on pony and trap. A stable was provided near to the church where horses were stalled for the duration of the service. Although Ernest loved to go to church, he was fascinated all the more so by the horses and eagerly watched as they arrived. It was a great environment in which to raise a young boy.

Mr. Hugh McKinty was the minister of the church and was well respected throughout the district. He was a quiet and godly man. He loved the Scriptures, and he was concerned for his flock. His character was greatly reflected in some of the comments that were often made about him in the local community. They said that when Hugh McKinty went to visit a family, this quiet man brought no news and took no news away. It was also well known that the minister wore hob nail boots. The people became aware of this because when Hugh McKinty visited a home and knelt down to pray with the family the large studs on the sole of the boots were clearly seen by all.

Mr. & Mrs. Allen and the family attended the Sabbath services regularly at the Annahilt church. Apart from these weekly services young Ernest also attended weddings, funerals and any other activity of the church. There was nothing more exciting for a boy to do in Annahilt.

Although the Allen family were church-goers, the most important impression left on Ernest as a boy were the prayers and Bible lessons which he learned at his mother's knee. Ernest remembers that every morning his mother began the day on her knees at an old wooden chair reading her Bible and spending time in prayer. In the evenings she gathered the children around the fireside and led the family in singing the songs from Alexander's little red hymn book.

Ernest was not sorry when he completed school and was able to get into long trousers and do a man's job. Although he would have enjoyed a farmer's life, Ernest showed interest in horticulture, and his first job was at Bradshaw's nursery at Hillsborough. Some time later he worked in Bell's nursery also in Hillsborough. These jobs involved working at the beautiful gardens at Hillsborough Castle which was the residence of the Governor of Northern Ireland.

One Sunday evening Ernest's boyhood friend William Radcliffe invited him to go to special gospel meetings which were being conducted in Hillsborough. William kindly offered, "Ernie, if you would like to go with me to the meeting, I will give you a lift." Ernie accepted his friend's offer. In those days few people had cars in that part of the country, so it was certainly not that kind of lift that William was offering. Instead, he arrived for Ernie and invited him to sit on the bar of the bicycle while he pedaled two miles to the mission in Hillsborough.

There was a large crowd present when the two boys arrived at the Friends' Meeting House in Park Street where the meetings were being held. When they arrived the congregation was already singing one of Alexander's hymns which Ernie had learned from his mother. The ride to the meeting had been uncomfortable, but as the service progressed Ernie began to feel a different kind of discomfort in his soul. In that meeting God began to answer Mrs. Allen's faithful prayers for her only son.

Ernie recalls his experience of conversion. "In that meeting I came under deep conviction of sin. Although I accepted a ride to the meeting on William Radcliffe's bicycle, I had to walk home alone. This gave me time to turn over in my mind and heart the things I had heard in the meeting. While walking on the narrow country road from Hillsborough to Annahilt I decided that I was going to be a Christian.

"These thoughts and that intended decision occupied my mind and raged in my heart every day. I continued to attend two meetings every week in Hillsborough. Finally, one Wednesday night six weeks later, Robert Anderson, the city missionary from Windsor City Mission, was preaching at the meeting. God continued to speak to my heart, and that night I was sure this was my last opportunity to accept Christ. I could resist Him no longer, and gladly I trusted the Lord Jesus Christ as my Saviour. I felt I was the chief of sinners, and the Scripture which the Holy Spirit used to give me the peace and joy of sins forgiven were in the words of Micah, 'Who is a God like unto Thee, that pardoneth iniquity. He retaineth not His anger forever, because He delighteth in mercy.' (Micah 7:18) I thought, If God delights in mercy, maybe He will have mercy on me. In trembling faith, I trusted in His Word.

"A short time after my conversion I was at a communion service for the first time. As I partook of the bread and wine, my heart was broken. I seemed to see the Lord Jesus suffering on the cross because of my sins. What a struggle I had trying to keep back the tears and not to break down crying before my friends. How I loved the Lord Jesus. Also in those days, I remember climbing up to the top of the hay in the hay shed, just to be alone with Him, to worship Him and to thank Him for saving a poor sinner like me."

Ernie's Christian development was greatly enhanced in 1935 when two Faith Mission Pilgrims, Miss Somerville and Miss Long, arrived in the district to conduct a Gospel Mission in a little hall known locally as "the Hut." The two ladies visited every house in the area travelling along the country roads either by foot or on bicycles. From the first night of the meetings God richly blessed the ministry of those two ladies, and people were converted. Amongst these converts were two brothers, Cecil and Morgan Greer who were Ernie's life-long friends.

When this mission was completed the Pilgrims moved nearby to Magheradartin to conduct another mission, and again many souls were saved and lives were transformed by the power of the gospel. After a month the lady evangelists moved to another locale near Annahilt, and these meetings were attended with similar times of blessing.

This work of grace was the talk of the country. Ernie and some friends were deeply challenged by the Pilgrims' dedication and longed to be involved in reaching out to win the lost for the Lord. So many people were converted in the Annahilt district that a Faith Mission Prayer Union was established at Edenticullo. This Prayer Union continues to this day under the leadership of Rex McClelland.

It was in Hillsborough that Ernie had his first experience of speaking in a public meeting. Many of the young Christian lads thought that if two lady Pilgrims could stand up and speak so well then they also would try it. Ernie was not of that persuasion; however, one night at the Christian Workers' Union Hall in Hillsborough, Ernie was invited to give his testimony. The experience was shattering. He loved the Lord, but he found it difficult to articulate how he felt, and with a few stammering words he related the date of his conversion. The duration of the testimony was extremely brief, and Ernie felt that neither the pulpit nor the platform was a place for him.

In the autumn of 1935 Mr. & Mrs. Allen and family decided they should move back to the Duncairn Gardens area of Belfast after many years of living in the country. For the parents it was returning home, but for Ernie it was a completely new experience. Besides finding a new job in Belfast, Ernie also had to find a new spiritual home. He found a position with Davenports of Belfast which allowed him to continue in horticultural work. The only contact that he had in respect of a spiritual home was the central Faith Mission Prayer Union which he began to attend.

At the Prayer Union he met Mr. Fred Sloan who invited him to attend the meetings at the Mustard Seed Mission in Vistula Street, just off the Crumlin Road. The Christians at the Mustard Seed made sure that the young man who had just come up from the country felt at home amongst them. Mr. & Mrs. John Govan, the founders of the Mustard Seed Mission, led the work at the Hall. The singing was bright; the preaching was fervent, and the prayer times were heart-warming.

Soon Ernie became involved in all the work of the Hall. He stood with them in the open-air meetings and often testified to what the Lord had done for him. He was given a class in the Sunday school and relished the opportunity to teach the Word of God. The weekly prayer meeting was a priority for Ernie, and with the others he would often pour out his heart to God for blessing on God's work.

One feature of the spiritual life at the Mustard Seed Mission that made a lasting impression on Ernie was the emphasis Mr. & Mrs. Govan gave to missionary work. They were closely associated with the Worldwide Evangelization Crusade, a mission founded by the former English cricketer and missionary pioneer C. T. Studd.

In the years that followed C. T. Studd's death in 1931 there was a steady stream of young volunteers who wished to follow the sacrifice of the founder of the WEC and serve God in distant mission fields. Not long after Ernie started to attend the Mustard Seed Mission there was a farewell service for Mr. & Mrs. William Weir as they left Northern Ireland to serve the Lord in India.

In July 1936, Mr. John Govan Jr. took a party of friends from Northern Ireland to visit the annual WEC Missionary Conference at the Bible College of Wales in Swansea. Ernie was invited to go. He did not know it then, but this conference was to change Ernie's life completely.

Christians had come from all over the British Isles to be present at these meetings. For Ernie it was a wonderful week. The conference hall at the college was packed to capacity. Mr. Norman Grubb, the general secretary of WEC and son-in-law of C. T. Studd, was the main speaker. Every day he gave challenging reports of what God was doing in the various mission fields and preached inspiring messages from the Word of God. Veteran missionaries and new candidates gave thrilling testimonies and challenging reports of their work. Mr. Pantridge had just returned from the Belgian Congo and recounted the moving story of his wife's death in the heart of Africa. For Ernie the whole week was a moving and life-changing experience.

On Friday morning, 17th July 1936 the conference hall was packed to capacity for the final meeting of the Missionary Conference. It had been a very emotional and impressionable week. Could Ernie ever be the same again? He vividly remembers that last meeting, "In that meeting God called me to give my life to His service. I knew that the Lord's return was near, and that dark times lay ahead for this world. God gave me a vision of a future world wide ministry of blessing. The Lord spoke to me and promised 'If you give your life to me I will give you a life of blessing.' I knelt in full and glad surrender to the Saviour.

"Two verses of a missionary hymn were a great challenge to me at that time:

Sound ye the trumpet call,
Heralds proclaim Jesus as Lord of all.
Sound forth His fame,
Lift high His kingly crown,
Tell of His great renown,
Let every knee bow down at His blessed Name.

Who will go forth for Him?
Who will arise, though eyes with tears are dim?
Severed loved ties,
Counting all things but loss,
Earth's highest gain but dross,
And glorying in the cross, who will arise?

"On my return home I found that my life had been radically changed, and I had to face up to all that was involved in obeying the call of God. The Scriptures challenged me, 'He that loveth father and mother more than Me, is not worthy of Me, and he that loveth son or daughter more than Me, is not worthy of Me, and he that taketh not his cross and followeth after Me, is not worthy of Me. If any man will come after Me, let him deny himself and take up his cross and follow Me. For whosoever will save his life shall lose it, and whosoever will lose his life for My sake, shall find it.'"

Back in Belfast Ernie continued his busy involvement with the work and witness of the Mustard Seed Mission Hall. As he matured in his Christian life he was encouraged by Mr. Govan to preach in the open-air meetings, and opportunities were given to him to give a message from the Scriptures at the weekly fellowship meetings.

These openings to serve the Lord were good experiences for young Ernie, but he was impatient to move out into the work of the gospel. He wanted to go into training for God's work immediately.

This aspiration was tempered by the wise counsel given to him that he should wait for God's time and to seek for the Lord's guidance.

When would the Lord open the door for Ernie, and where was God leading him?

Chapter Three

MUSTARD SEED FAITH

Moving up to Belfast from the farmlands of County Down had been a big step for Ernie, but he soon found his feet in the city. However, to take God's leading and step out of his employment, leave home and trust God to supply all of his needs was another matter. Ernie needed to be sure that the Lord was in this step. How could he be sure?

Ernie had no doubt about the growing conviction he felt in his heart that he should go to Bible College to prepare for future service. The burden in his heart made him restless in his employment, and although he was serving the Lord at the Mustard Seed Mission Hall he felt there was more that he should be doing to win the lost for Jesus Christ. It seemed that when he read the Scriptures they were urging him to step out and trust God. When he knelt in prayer for his quiet time with the Lord, the conviction only intensified.

Ernie wanted to be certain of God's leading in his life. He thought of Gideon who had asked the Lord for a definite sign. Should he ask the Lord for such a sign to confirm what he already felt in his heart was God's will? Ernie "put out the fleece" and asked the Lord that if He wanted him to go to the Bible College of Wales in Swansea to give him a definite token. He told no one of his dealings with God, but Ernie was not surprised when the Lord honoured that token. There was joy in his heart for the assurance that God was opening a door for him.

Ernie's delight in discovering that God wanted him to go to Wales was tempered by the implications of leaving his mother and father and sisters. He had always enjoyed the security of his home and to leave it was probably the hardest thing Ernie had experienced in his life up to that time. Nonetheless, he had made his decision to follow God's leading, and there was no turning back.

Ernie sailed from Belfast docks on 19th September 1938. He found that his arrival at the Bible College was a humbling experience. The college campus was impressive. There was a lot of activity with visiting missionaries and speakers coming for short visits. The dedication of those he met touched Ernie greatly.

The Bible College of Wales is located in a leafy upper class suburb east of Swansea and near to Mumbles Beach. The school was founded by Rees Howells who was known as "The Director." The college campus was comprised of two large mansion houses on either side of the road, called Derwen Fawr and Sketty. Surrounding the two houses were a series of out-buildings some of which were stables which had been converted into workshops and dormitories. The spacious and well kept gardens were networked by a series of paths between the various houses. On the grounds there was also a conference hall and a small hospital.

Just down the road from the Bible college was the Emmanuel Grammar School where over eighty missionary children boarded while their parents served the Lord in various parts of the world. One hundred people lived at the college, and all were living by faith. Ernie felt he had come to live amongst spiritual giants. Ernie knew that he had stepped out to trust the Lord to meet his personal needs, but to run a college this size by faith just amazed him. This was exactly why he had come to Swansea - so he could learn from men and women of faith and come to know the Lord in a deeper sense and to study God's Word.

Ernie soon fitted into the routine of college life, but he discovered that life at Bible college was not all to do with academics. In addition to the studies and lectures in the morning, afternoon and evening, the students had to scrub floors, tend gardens, peel potatoes, wash dishes and what seemed like another hundred other chores. There was little spare time. Nearly every evening the meeting or lecture developed into an extended prayer meeting.

The Director gave devotional talks to the students most days, and he was ably supported by very dedicated and efficient members of staff. Their lives and lectures made a great impact on Ernie's life. Of that time Ernie recalls, "After I had settled into the college routine, my chief concern was to have fellowship with God, to get to know my Bible and to grow in faith. I wanted to obtain answers to prayer and to learn what was the Lord's will for my life in the future. From the first, I was cast upon the Lord, and graciously He answered prayer and assured me that I was in the centre of His will."

During this time there were ominous signs of impending war all over Europe. There was great concern at the college about the worsening situation in the nation and across the world, and this became a focus of their prayers. When the Prime Minister, Mr. Neville Chamberlain, declared war against Nazi Germany in September 1939, everybody's life was affected.

Staff and students engaged in concentrated days of prayer and fasting. Many students had to engage in various forms of war time service whilst they remained in college. Ernie, with his background in gardening was put in charge of the college grounds. He supervised the work of some of the men who were engaged in wartime service.

After his first year at Swansea, Ernie returned to Belfast for a visit. There was no way for him to realise then that he would not be returning home again for some years. Ernie's original plan had been to spend only two years at college. The Lord's plan for Ernie was not only different than he thought, but it was for the best. Ernie's college experience developed into ten years. Although these years had their frustrating times, God used them to deepen Ernie's burden and shape his life for future ministry.

Ernie's next visit to Belfast was when he received the sad news that his mother had passed away. He held onto all the cherished memories he had of his mother and thanked God for the lady who made such a great impression upon his life. Her prayers had brought him to Jesus Christ, and in answer to her intercession he was in Christian service.

The new circumstances brought about in Wales because of the duration of war gave Ernie an opportunity to engage in more concentrated Bible study and the reading of church history. He was not only enriched by more precious insights into God's Word, but the college library provided him with access to many biographies of great men of God. He read volume after volume, and these stirred his soul more and more. He felt he was sitting at the feet of the great reformers, evangelists and missionary leaders and learning first hand from their experiences with God and their exploits for Him. These spiritual giants of the past made a lasting impact on Ernie's life.

These historical biographies were read against the back drop of what was going on in Europe, the Middle East, North Africa, the Far East and the Americas. Ernie's soul was stretched. He longed and hungered for great revival such as God had sent in former times. With such a burden on his heart Ernie decided to read only biographies and writings of men of God who had been endued with power from on high and whose ministry had resulted in the salvation of precious souls.

The more Ernie read the more he felt that others should learn of these revivals and of the men God used. Dr. K. Priddy, who was a great and godly man and principal of the Emmanuel School, loaned Ernie his type-writer. Ernie soon mastered the keyboard and began to type out summary accounts of the great revivals of former years. In any spare time he could find Ernie laboured over the type-writer to produce a record of great spiritual awakenings. These summaries formed the basis of the first booklets that Ernie produced and sent to men involved in the ministry.

Ernie is still stirred and motivated by these heroes of the faith who made a profound influence on his life. It was chiefly the Protestant Reformers and their costly stand for Biblical truth that helped Ernie settle his convictions in the unchanging doctrines of the gospel of Jesus Christ. He highlighted his reasons why they influenced him:

JOHN WYCLIFFE

In the dark night of the fourteenth century, when the world was lying in the lap of the Devil, John Wickcliffe shone forth as the Morning Star of the Reformation. He was removed from the position of authority as Oxford's Professor of Divinity and branded as an instrument of the Devil and the author of division. However, he won world acclaim for his scholarly translation of the Scriptures into the English language. That translation made the Bible accessible to the common people and brought to all who read it, the good news of God's saving grace.

He was driven into exile by an alliance of church and state. He knew well these same hypocritical masters would unite to destroy his translation of the Bible. Therefore, in spite of all their malicious threats and evil schemes against him, he not only stood for the truth, but mobilised the Lollards, his students, who went up and down the length of England proclaiming the gospel.

MARTIN LUTHER

The Spirit of God used Martin Luther to open the doors of the mighty arsenal of God's Word in order that the soldiers of Christ in coming generations might be well armed for the conflict with the powers of darkness. He brought to light the great doctrines of the Faith that had been hidden in ecclesiastical darkness for centuries. Through the circulation of the Scriptures and the reformed doctrines Europe was awakened to the Reformation.

JOHN CALVIN

Through reading the Bible in French John Calvin became a wholehearted follower of the Reformed Faith. Within a short time he became a leader of the Protestants in Paris. In 1541 the citizens of Geneva asked Calvin to come and help them. For over twenty years he laboured to make Geneva a city of God where he taught great biblical truths.

JOHN KNOX - SCOTLAND'S DELIVERER

If ever the man and the hour struck together it was when John Knox landed in Scotland in 1559. The effect of his preaching changed history and brought "root and branch reform." Of John Knox the English Ambassador wrote, "He is able in one hour to put more life in us than five hundred trumpets blustering in our ears." John Knox found Scotland in darkness, and he gave her light. When Scotland was incarcerated in the dark superstition of Romanism, Knox emancipated her, gave her liberty.

Reading, re-reading and typing out these stirring accounts, widened Ernie's vision and burdened his heart deeply. Not everyone understood Ernie's vision. Although he shared his concerns with the leaders of God's work they did not share Ernie's enthusiasm for what God had put on his heart. However, the fact that it was God who placed the burden on him is what gave Ernie the encouragement to press on.

The prolonged time at Swansea also brought many valuable lessons on the discipline of his Christian life. The life of faith became his way of life. He learned to walk with God and see God supply his needs. All during the years of the war Ernie along with other members of staff at Swansea trusted God to supply their daily needs. Ernie personally was trusting the Lord for the day-to-day necessities of life without sharing with anyone that he was in need.

Perhaps the greatest lesson Ernie had to learn was to wait on God. When his earnest prayers did not bring the expected answer, it was a matter of waiting on God. When it seemed that God delayed in opening a door for the future, Ernie had to wait on God. Impatience at times provoked longings to move ahead, but the servant of God had to learn that the Spirit's restraint was just as important and as essential as His constraint. Delays and denials proved valuable lessons in the school of spiritual experience and maturity.

All of these experiences were intensely personal for Ernie, and they laid a good foundation for the work for which God was planning and preparing him. Without the prolonged period of time at Swansea, Ernie would not have been ready for what God had in store for him.

The end of the Second World War brought a new emphasis to college life at Swansea. The days of intercession for the war were concluded, and many who had been there since before the war began started to move into other ministries. A new door began to swing open for God's servant, Ernie Allen.

Chapter Four

Revival Is Practical

Reading not only exercises the mind, it also provokes and stimulates the soul. When Paul was confined to a Roman cell he wanted his books, and especially the parchments brought to him. John Wesley, one of Ernie Allen's heroes, said, "Either read or get out of the ministry."

Ernie Allen had no difficulty in agreeing with John Wesley on this point. He was completely at home among books. They were his mentors and inspiration. For nearly ten years the writings of reformers and revivalists were the tools God used to stimulate, stir and shape His servant to be content with nothing less than revival. He longed for the enduement of the power of the Holy Spirit on his own life and on the ministry of fellow preachers and saw it as the only answer to the ills and apathy of the times.

Just as Ernie's belief in the great doctrines of the Christian faith had been nurtured and strengthened by imbibing the history of leaders of the Protestant Reformation, so also his study of the great revivalists of former years made an impression on his life. These accounts of great men gave him a hunger for similar times of refreshing from the presence of the Lord. Some of these servants of God not only left their mark on Ernie, but they became his role models for future years in God's work. Ernie later wrote of these men:

> These are the men who fired my soul and gave me a passionate burden for revival in our time: John Wesley and George Whitefield. God stemmed the tide of sin and darkness in England in the eighteenth century through these two men and their co-workers. They were men endued with power from on high. John Wesley said on January 1, 1739, "Mr. Hall, Kinchin, Ingham, Whitefield, Hutchins and my brother Charles were present at our love-feast in Fetter Lane with about sixty of our brethren. At three in the morning, as we were continuing instant in prayer, the power of God came mightily upon us, insomuch that many cried out for exceeding joy, and many fell to the ground. As soon as we were recovered a little from that awe and amazement at the presence of His Majesty, we broke out with one voice, 'We praise Thee, O God, we acknowledge Thee to be the Lord.'"
>
> When George Whitefield was twenty-four years old he was preaching to twenty thousand grim colliers at Kingswood, Bristol. Referring to these great occasions, he wrote, "The day was fine, the sun shone very bright; and the people, standing in such awful manner around the mount, in the profoundest silence, filled me with holy admiration. Having no righteousness of their own to renounce, they were glad to hear of Jesus, who was a Friend to publicans, and who came to call not the righteous but sinners to repentance. The first discovery of their being affected was to see the white gutters made by their tears, which plentifully fell down their black cheeks."
>
> For the next thirty-four years Whitefield's preaching stirred many parts of the British Isles and the American

States also. His coworker was Jonathan Edwards who also was instrumental in the New England revival.

John Wesley also joined Whitefield at Kingswood, and there he preached his first sermon in the open air. Wesley began to look upon all the world as his parish, and for fifty years he preached almost daily to crowds of five to twenty thousand people. In his ministry he travelled a quarter of a million miles - mostly on horseback and preached forty thousand sermons.

Early in his work Wesley resolved not to strike a blow in any place where he could not follow the blow. As soon as he had won a soul from the devil's ranks, he enlisted him in his own, and arranged for his training and employment in the campaign of soul-winning.

Wesley also realised the importance of raising a generation of well instructed saints. His preachers were supplied with books which they were bound to study; he organised different grades of classes for his followers; and he issued four hundred publications for the instruction and enlightenment of his people.

Charles Grandison Finney was twenty-six when he began to study law, and it was at this time his spiritual experience began. The Holy Spirit was upon him for a long time, showing him his sinfulness and guilt. He was thoroughly under conviction of sin. One morning in the Autumn of 1821 the crisis came. He cried out to God for mercy. God heard him and showed him the way of salvation through the Lord Jesus Christ. That was the greatest day of his life. He entered into peace with God, and in the evening he received a mighty baptism of the Holy Spirit. From that time Finney knew that he was called by God to be an evangelist. It was in that calling he was most outstanding. For fifty years mighty revivals of religion broke forth under his ministry. One of the most notable of those revivals happened in the city of Rochester,

New York. The Holy Spirit worked so mightily in the high school that nearly every teacher and student was converted. As a result of these conversions, forty of those students became ministers of the gospel, and a large number of them became foreign missionaries. One hundred thousand of the converts of that revival joined local churches.

Later in life Finney became President of Oberlin College, and during those years twenty thousand students came under his influence and inspiration.

Finney made one of his most forthright statements when he spoke about the renewal of the image of Jesus in Christians:

"The renewal of the image of Jesus Christ in Christians is God's natural and God's exclusive means for the convicting and the conversion of sinners and the reviving of His work. The first powerful action upon lost sinners is the look, and the earnest deportment of Christians. This is the result of the renewal of the first love to our Lord Jesus Christ in Christians.

"Remember, before the world can be moved, we must have the image of Jesus renewed in ourselves. Backslidden Christians must be brought to repentance, and every sin abandoned. We must rise into a holy life.

"Frequent seasons of Bible reading and secret prayer are wholly indispensable in keeping up communion with God. Spend much time every day and every night in prayer and communion with God.

"This will make you a power for salvation. No amount of learning and study can compensate for the loss of this communion with God. If you fail to maintain communion with God, you are as weak as another man."

The '59 Revival swept around the English speaking world. From 1856 to 1866 the English speaking world experienced one of the greatest revivals of religion in history. We often hear of the '57-'58 revival in America, and of the '59 revival in Ireland and Wales; but the revival movement of those years was something that touched nearly every country in the world. In this great movement of the Spirit of God thousands of great evangelistic meetings were conducted, and a new stream of spiritual life flowed through the churches.

The blessing came to Ireland through the prayers of four young farmers and to Wales through two young ministers. Everywhere the revival touched it was followed by the forming of prayer groups, until over two million persons joined the churches on both sides of the Atlantic.

So impressed was Ernie with these men of God and workings of the Holy Spirit that as he prayed and waited on God, a thought came to him. He felt God impressed upon him that if literature was the instrument God used to arouse his appetite for revival then surely the Lord could use revival literature to awaken others.

Motivated by this constraint, Ernie compiled several booklets of messages by Charles G. Finney and wrote off to various printers for an estimated price for publishing them in booklet form. A printer in Nelson, Lancashire, came up with the most favourable bid. Having trusted and proved God to meet his personal needs Ernie remembered the words of Hudson Taylor, "God's work done in God's way will not lack God's supply." God honoured Ernie's faith and provided the funds to publish his first booklet.

The unerring hand of his Sovereign Lord was pointing Ernie in a direction that would eventually develop into a worldwide ministry. That first revival publication was only the embryo of millions of booklets in multiple languages. It was the early bud that would blossom into a very fruitful ministry.

It was in April 1948 that Ernie produced his first publication of thirty-six pages under the associate agency, The Revival Publishing Company. Ernie published several thousand of the first edition which contained a message by the American revivalist, Charles G. Finney; "The Spiritual Preparation of a Soul Winner". To Ernie, "The Revival Series" seemed to be the obvious name for the booklets.

As Ernie became more involved in this ministry he realised some practical matters needed to be considered. He was not at liberty to use the Bible College address as a return contact for sending out the booklets, so he approached an old friend back in Belfast, Mr. Fred Sloan. Fred had introduced Ernie to the Mustard Seed Mission Hall and had remained a firm friend during Ernie's absence from Northern Ireland. Fred and his wife agreed to allow Ernie to use their Ligoneil residence as a contact address, and they also volunteered to wrap and mail the orders.

Advertisements for the booklets were placed in Christian magazines and periodicals, and there was an encouraging response. At that time the booklets sold for the nominal charge of one shilling. Soon orders began to flood into the Sloans' address, and Fred and his wife were busy filling envelopes, wrapping parcels and dispatching orders all over Britain. Requests for booklets began to come from as far away as the United States, Canada and Australia.

The favourable sale of the first edition encouraged Ernie to produce a second booklet which was largely financed by the proceeds of the first one. The pattern of supply and demand continued until Ernie produced a series of seven booklets, six of which consisted of messages by Charles G. Finney and the seventh being Ernie's own publication, "The History of Revivals of Religion". Dr. Oswald J. Smith, noted Canadian pastor and author, wrote the foreword for the last booklet.

When all seven booklets were in circulation advertisements were placed in many magazines including the Salvation Army's War Cry and the Keswick Convention's magazine, The Life of Faith. The advertisement read:

As the number of publications increased so did the demand for the booklets. After publishing the third booklet, "Instructions for Young Converts", the request for more books became too much for Mr. & Mrs. Sloan who had faithfully worked attending to orders and sending packets off daily from the local post office. Reluctantly they decided to relinquish their role in the distribution of the booklets.

Their decision to withdraw put pressure on Ernie who was still resident at the Bible College in Swansea. He found it impossible to remain there and continue the ministry that the Lord was prospering and enlarging. His decision to leave Swansea was not easy, nevertheless, God was calling and Ernie had no alternative but to say good-bye to those with whom he had been associated through his years at Swansea.

Upon his return to Northern Ireland Ernie went to live in Lisburn with his father and two sisters, Elizabeth and Jessie. Immediately upon arrival Ernie assumed the responsibility of attending to the orders that came in from all over the world. One remarkable letter came from Salvation Army Commissioner Couts, the leader of the Army in Australia and New Zealand and grandson of seafaring Captain John Couts whose life was completely transformed by the power of the gospel. Commissioner Couts requested that Mr. Allen send all seven booklets in the "Revival Series" to every Salvation Army officer in Australia and New Zealand.

The first edition of this initial series sold out quickly, and the booklets made an impact on many lives. Letters flowed in from Christians far and near expressing how they shared Ernie's burden for revival. Revival to Ernie Allen was much more than the subject of a sermon, the emotion of a meeting or something that was organised by human minds. He agreed with Charles G. Finney who said, "Revival is nothing else than a new beginning of obedience to God...

a deep repentance, a breaking down of heart, a getting down into the dust before God with deep humility, and a forsaking of sin."

Now that he was resident back in Northern Ireland, he was free to devote all his time to "The Revival Movement" ministry. Ernie began to accept invitations to speak at churches, halls and conferences. Ernie Allen is a soft spoken man, both in and out of the pulpit. His preaching was not characterised by thundering and barraging shouts. His quiet manner and persuasive ministry reflected his passion for revival which was essentially a passion for the lost. He sincerely believed that revival which was divorced from evangelism and the reaching of the lost was not true revival.

Hundreds of letters started to arrive from all over the world at Ernie's Lisburn address. Many people requested more booklets, and others gave reports of blessing and salvation. Spontaneously many wrote asking to be included as members of the Revival Movement. One such request came from an African pastor in the Gold Coast, Ghana.

Dear Christian Workers,

Loving greetings in the precious name of Jesus! Having received one of your revival booklets from a Christian friend of mine, I went through it and received inspiration, and it moved me to write and join you as a soul-winner. I therefore desire you to forward me seven booklets of your "Revival Series."

I wish to be a member of the Revival Movement. Pray for me to become a soul-winner for Jesus in the Gold Coast.

Yours ever in Jesus.

Such requests from abroad coupled with the local interest in the Revival Movement, prompted Ernie to set up what became known as the "The Worldwide Revival Movement."

In association with this organisation, Ernie published the first edition of a quarterly magazine which was simply called, The Revival Movement. The pilot edition of the periodical gave a report of the first meeting of the newly formed Worldwide Revival Movement. It stated:

> The inaugural meeting and tea of the Worldwide Revival Movement was held on 19th January, 1952 in the Lombard Cafe, Belfast. The chairman and host was Mr. William J. Morgan, M.P. Addresses were given by the founder and secretary, Mr. W. E. Allen, the honourable vice-president, Mr. T. McKibben, Mr. H. J. Mateer, Mr. David Shepherd and others.
>
> This movement has grown out of the work of the Revival Publishing Company, which publishes the seven "Revival Series" booklets which are rapidly becoming recognised as text books on this subject. The first six of these books are by Charles G. Finney, the world famous Revivalist, and contain an outline of his writings.
>
> Mr. Allen spoke with special reference to the words, "In the last days, saith God, I will pour out My Spirit upon all flesh." He then referred to many times in the last 300 years when God literally poured His Spirit on multitudes of people, as in the great revivals of 1857-59. He was led, he said, to begin the publishing branch of this work about four years ago, with the aim of instructing and building up young Christians to be efficient witnesses for Christ, and soul-winners, in their own church or community all over the world. Since then about 60,000 of these books have gone throughout the world, to the British Isles, the Middle East, India, Australia, New Zealand, South Africa, East Africa, West Africa, United States of America, Canada and many other countries. He mentioned that some Bible colleges are beginning to use the booklets as text books. One college recently sent for 1050 publications.

"However," he said, "Literature alone will not promote revival, God must raise up men in every country who will lead the young Christians all over the world in the campaign of soul-winning and worldwide evangelisation. Men with the burden and vision of revival are needed to form classes and groups which will study these books, and carry out their instructions, working for a revival where they are. Many such groups are now being formed."

The Revival Movement gave account of great revivals including reports from the continuing revival in the Isle of Lewis and contained stirring messages on revival and soul-winning from current evangelists and those greatly used in past generations. One notice that appeared in the first edition simply stated, "There is no membership fee to pay or form to complete in order to join the Revival Movement. All who use the "Revival Series" booklets and receive the magazine are naturally members of the movement."

Following the publication of the "Revival Series", the quarterly magazine struck a chord with many pastors, preachers and Christian people. Subscriptions and requests for the periodical exceeded all expectations.

Here is a typical letter from a minister who wrote at that time:

Dear Mr. Allen,

I was very pleased to receive a copy of your magazine, The Revival Movement. The reading of it has thrilled my soul. I am at one with you in the desires and thoughts expressed and the longing for a Holy Spirit visitation. You will be interested to know that I have given my people a number of addresses on this most vital theme. In addition to my regular church prayer meetings, two cottage prayer meetings to pray for revival began about twelve months ago and are still well attended.

> A number of my young people are going out as witnesses, preaching the Word. On a recent Sunday one of them had the joy of seeing twenty-nine conversions. Last Sunday one of my Sunday School teachers had seven of her class accept the Saviour. I pray that what you have begun may spread, bringing a greater devotion to the Master. If I can do anything to further the Movement, I shall be delighted to do so, that He may be glorified.

Ernie sent copies of the magazine and booklets to Dr. Oswald J. Smith, pastor of the People's Church, Toronto, Canada, and internationally known evangelist. Dr. Smith showed great interest in the Movement and entered into correspondence with Ernie. Subsequently he accepted an invitation to become the honorary president of the Worldwide Revival Movement. The following announcement appeared in the magazine.

> From the beginning of this work one of my greatest encouragements has been in the fellowship and help of Dr. Oswald J. Smith, of the People's Church, Toronto, Canada. In the midst of his unique worldwide ministry in the cause of revival, missions, and world evangelisation, he has taken time to help forward this new work in many ways. His articles in the magazine have been a most valuable contribution and a blessing to many people.
>
> During the past eighteen months we have contacted new Christian friends in many countries. Some of them have asked, "Who are the leaders of the Worldwide Revival Movement?" It became clear that we needed a leader who is known to embody the vision and burden of the movement, and it is a great joy to announce that Dr. Smith has agreed to act as our President. We are more than grateful to Dr. Smith, and we also thank God for all this means for the future of the work. Already Dr. Smith's appointment as president had a real influence in the

beginning of a new venture of publishing our revival literature in Europe."

Among these developments in his ministry other significant things were happening in Ernie's life at this time. In June 1952 Ernie accompanied a group of young people from Lisburn to attend the annual Portstewart Convention on the north shores of Co. Londonderry. Besides enjoying the rich ministry of internationally known Bible expositors under the large canvas tent, Ernie had another meeting that would give him a different sort of stirring in his heart and would change his life.

At the guest house where the Lisburn party stayed, there was a young lady who had come up from Portavogie, Co. Down, to attend the convention. Kathleen Hull arrived in Portstewart alone but entered into the fellowship and friendship of the Christian friends from Lisburn who were staying at the same guest house. As the week progressed some of the Lisburn girls remarked to Kathleen that Ernie Allen was paying a lot of attention to her. During the meal times and in the fellowship gatherings at the house, Kathleen became aware that Ernie was very friendly towards her, and by the end of the week he asked for her address.

Ernie was single minded in the work God had called him to, but he knew that the Lord would direct him to the right partner. As in all other areas of his life, he not only prayed about it, but he learned to commit the matter to the Lord and wait for Him. When Ernie met Kathleen he not only liked her, but also felt the Lord was prompting him to pursue this matter.

After the convention finished and the friends returned home, Ernie wrote to Kathleen. Even though there was a lot of mail to be attended to for the Revival Movement ministry, the correspondence between Lisburn and Portavogie rapidly increased. Soon the friendship that was formed in Portstewart blossomed into courtship.

Kathleen Hull had been converted as an eleven-year-old girl through the ministry of Faith Mission Pilgrims. Not only was she brought to Christ through these dedicated ladies, but Kathleen was challenged to dedicate her life to the Lord Jesus Christ. She felt she could never be a preacher, but prayed that the Lord would lead her to a partner who would involve her in Christian work. Little did she know how God would do far more than she ever imagined.

Neither Ernie nor Kathleen owned a car; consequently the distance between Lisburn and Portavogie put them at a distinct disadvantage. However, love always finds a way in every circumstance. Kathleen travelled every day on the bus into Belfast where she was employed as a civil servant. Ernie made a point of meeting her and spending some time with her during the evenings after she had finished work. Apart from seeing each other on the occasional weekend, the young courting couple continued with this arrangement for fifteen months.

When it became clear that their relationship was in the will of God, and it was going to result in marriage, there were matters which Kathleen had to face. At that time a single girl employed as a civil servant was made redundant upon marrying. Marriage for Kathleen therefore would mean stepping out of secular employment and stepping into a life of faith with Ernie. Since 1938 Ernie had trusted the Lord to meet all his needs, and he had proved that the Lord never fails. Kathleen's introduction to this lifestyle was a big step, but she was prepared to trust the Lord with her husband.

On September 30th 1953, Ernie and Kathleen were married by Mr. S. Stevenson at Glastry Presbyterian Church near Portavogie. Together they set up home at 95 Omeath Street in East Belfast.

After Kathleen ceased to work for Her Majesty's government she became the first book-keeper for the Revival Movement. Ernie transferred all his literature from his father's home in Lisburn to their new home, and he was soon busy producing and circulating booklets and magazines once again. While most houses in the area furnished their front room, commonly called "the parlour" for visitors, Ernie and Kathleen's "parlour" was transformed into a book depot and office.

The periodical that appeared on the same month in which the happy couple tied the knot, appropriately contained a testimony of Ernie's burden for revival and reasons to continue his work.

> In 1936 God called me to devote my life to the evangelisation of the world. During the years that followed He led me to study the great revivals of the past and the influence they had on the spread of the Gospel. Living for years in the Word of God and under the teaching of the Holy Spirit, and looking on the struggles, prayers, labours, and triumphs of men like Wycliffe, Tyndale, Luther, and those who followed them, I began to see that the greatest days of the Church had been the days of revival. Every movement that has blessed the world originated from vital blessing in some soul.
>
> One thing that stands out in the story of every revival is the wonderful influence that ordinary well-instructed Christians exerted. Such Christians and young converts, through their changed lives, testimonies and prayers, brought the presence of God, and the conviction of eternal realities to bear powerfully on the minds of sinners. It was the contact of such Christians with the world that spread the blessing.
>
> During this period God inspired my own heart with the vision of a worldwide army of soul-winners who could promote revivals of religion in every country, and He called me to the work of raising this army. How could this be done? He led me to publish some of the writings of Charles G. Finney, which have been so wonderfully used of God, in six booklets called, "The Revival Series". These comprise a course on soul-winning and revival work. The seventh booklet is the "History of Revivals of Religion" by myself, with a foreword by Dr. Oswald J. Smith who wrote in the foreword, "I know of only one or two Bible schools where a course of study is offered on the history of

> Evangelism and Revival, and nothing is more needed. Moreover, there are hardly any text books on the subject. I am glad, therefore, that Mr. W. E. Allen has attempted to meet this need."

Besides Ernie's confidence in the power of the printed page he also appreciated the importance of great preaching. While there were gifted and powerful preachers locally, Ernie read of men whose ministry God had greatly blessed in other parts of the world.

Ernie received several reports from the islands of Northwest Scotland of the genuine revival that was taking place there through the powerful ministry of Duncan Campbell. Early in 1953 Ernie invited Duncan Campbell to Northern Ireland, and of these meetings Ernie wrote:

> It was my privilege to arrange a series of meetings in Northern Ireland for Duncan Campbell. The meetings were convened from the 10th to the 18th of January, 1953 and were organised in connection with the Revival Movement.
>
> The burden of his visit was to tell the story of the Isle of Lewis Revival in order to stir up prayer for revival in our country. The first meeting was held in Belfast on the 10th. It was specially arranged to give laymen and Christian leaders an opportunity to hear his wonderful story. We were all deeply moved in that meeting as he spoke of how God prepared him for his part in the revival some weeks before it commenced. He told of how the revival continues; just the day before he left for Ireland he received an urgent call to return to Lewis as the revival had broken out afresh in a new district.
>
> During the next days great crowds attended the meetings in Lisburn, Lurgan, Banbridge and Ballymena. When we arrived at the Ballymena meeting the place was crowded. I never saw a building so tightly packed. Ballymena was a place mightily blessed in the '59 Revival, and God stirred

our hearts that night with the vision of a new awakening.

On Thursday morning Mr. Campbell addressed one of the most remarkable meetings of the Campaign. In the YMCA, Belfast, about 170 ministers of different denominations gathered to hear the story of the Revival in Lewis. We all listened with subdued hearts, very conscious of the presence of God. This meeting caused a great stir among the ministers. One result of it was that Mr. Campbell was invited to speak at the Portstewart Convention in June.

In the evening of that day Mr. Campbell addressed about 700 people in the First Presbyterian Church in Ballynahinch, and again the presence of God was very manifest. On Friday morning we set off for the historic City of Londonderry; there we met some of the leading Christians and were entertained most kindly by Mr. J. Goligher, who was responsible for the arrangements in connection with the meeting there that evening. Here again we experienced the same inspiring moving of the Holy Spirit. Friends came from as far as Milford, Co. Donegal, and a good number of students from Magee College were present.

On Saturday morning we left Londonderry for Portadown. Here Mr. Campbell addressed forty-six ministers of different denominations at a special meeting in the afternoon. In the evening he spoke to a crowded audience in the First Presbyterian Church. It was estimated that there were about 1,200 present. This was one of the most remarkable meetings of the series, and for weeks afterwards reports were received of persons who were very definitely blessed in this service. On Sunday, 18th, Mr. Campbell addressed his last meeting with us in Belfast.

It was a great privilege to enjoy the fellowship of Mr. Campbell. The more I came to know him the more I loved and respected him. He himself is the embodiment of what he preaches, and that is what gives power to his words.

Ernie felt constrained to invite some American evangelists to Northern Ireland, but to bring preachers from a distance was a great step of faith as international travel at this time was extremely expensive. Kathleen and other friends stood with Ernie to believe that the Lord would supply the need when he issued an invitation to evangelists who were being greatly used by God in the United States.

Harvey Springer was the first to accept an invitation to visit Northern Ireland and conduct special evangelistic meetings. God richly blessed the evangelist's ministry at Belfast's Wellington Hall and the visit proved to be a valuable investment for the Kingdom of God.

The success of Harvey Springer's visit encouraged Ernie to invite others. Dr. Oswald J. Smith, president of the Worldwide Revival Movement, made a return visit to Belfast following his very successful evangelistic mission at McQuiston Memorial Presbyterian Church in 1947. As on the previous visit, Dr. Smith preached with great anointing of the Holy Spirit, and many were converted.

Oswald J. Smith's visit was followed by other crusades conducted by John Coleman, who became the pastor of Banbridge Baptist Church, and Johnny Bisagno. All these visiting evangelists drew large crowds to the Wellington Hall and to other churches both in Belfast and provincial towns.

Among those who trusted the Lord Jesus Christ as Saviour at Johnny Bisagno's meetings in Roslyn Street Hall, was Stanley Barnes, a young man from that very street. Stanley not only entered missionary training, but after a short spell in Spain, he entered the ministry of the Free Presbyterian Church. Stanley, who has been a minister for twenty-seven years in Hillsborough, has been one of Ernie's close friends since his conversion.

Ernie organised prayer meetings for many who had identified with the Revival Movement. He forged a friendship and supported the ministry of a young man on the Ravenhill Road who also had a passion for revival and was being greatly used of God in evangelistic preaching. Ernie's friendship with Ian Paisley grew deeper as they shared the burden God had placed on their hearts. In turn Ian Paisley greatly encouraged Ernie in the Revival Movement's ministry.

During ten years of revival ministry, Ernie never forgot the early promise God had given him, "If you give your life to me I will give you a life of blessing." The fifties had been a decade of blessing. Over a hundred thousand booklets and magazines were circulating in many countries, and they presented a challenge to Christians to seek God for revival. Reports came from all around the world of people who had been blessed by the reading of the "Revival Series" booklets.

Their house on Omeath Street was more than a home - it was a centre for evangelism and a place where many came to share their burden with Ernie and Kathleen for blessing on God's work. It was not easy for a wife to keep a home that was partly a residence, a book depot, a circulation centre and the Revival Movement's office.

Added to all this, Ernie and Kathleen were greatly blessed when their daughter Heather was born in 1958. This was followed by a double blessing of twin boys, Paul and Clive, in 1959. The limited premises and the expanded family sharing a residence with all the literature, really brought pressure to the Allen home. However, Kathleen, who was a great help and encouragement to Ernie in the work, had gained a lot of experience in this life of faith. She had learned to trust the Lord not only to supply all their needs but to show the way ahead.

Although the booklets and gospel crusades had brought much blessing, nevertheless, Ernie's heart yearned to be more effective for the Lord and to be able to reach beyond his native Province. Could there still be more blessing? Ernie prayed for God to open other doors.

Chapter Five

OpeN DoorS

Opportunity often reveals great men in small places. Opportunities and challenges were beckoning Ernie to widen the ministry of the Revival Movement, but he waited on the Lord to open the right doors. As we will see shortly the door that opened was quite unexpected. On some weekends Ernie helped a fellowship of believers in East Belfast. He was subsequently appointed to the pastoral care of this small congregation. He was grateful for the new experience of consecutive ministry in the pulpit and the pastoral care of the people.

For the next two years Ernie dedicated his time to the continuing work of the Revival Movement as well as to the church in East Belfast, and God blessed both ministries. People were saved, and young converts greatly benefited from Ernie's ministry as the small congregation steadily grew. Ernie and Kathleen loved the fellowship of their friends in the church.

One evening Ernie led a young man, John Leebody, and his girlfriend, Elizabeth French, to the Lord Jesus Christ as Saviour.

Later Ernie considered it a privilege to be invited to officiate at the young couple's wedding. A special bond formed between Ernie and John and Elizabeth has remained firm over the years. John has been the honorary treasurer of the Revival Movement Association for many years, and his brother Alex Leebody and his wife have been faithful helpers of the Every Home Crusade

Ernie continued to feel the same challenge he had first experienced while studying the biographies of his historical heroes. Reformers and revivalists had inflamed his soul with zeal and burden for a revival of true religion. Other biographies challenged him about worldwide evangelisation. Even though Ernie had set out for college with the mission field on his mind, the Lord placed upon him a conviction about revival which was allied to evangelism.

Ernie wrote of the characters who left an imprint on his life and inspired him to reach out to the needy world around.

> I was always stirred to read of the zeal and sacrifice of great missionaries throughout the years. There were two who made the greatest impression.

COUNT ZINZENDORF AND THE MORAVIANS' MISSIONARY VISION

> At the time of their great revival there were only a few hundred of the Moravians, but they became possessed with the burden and vision of giving the Gospel to the whole world. In August, 1732, the first three men left for the West Indies. In their brown coats and their quaint hats, with bundles on their backs, and but thirty shillings in their pockets, no one who saw them would have thought that they were the pioneers of the great modern world-wide missionary movement, but they were.
>
> John Wesley was converted through the Moravians, and he visited Herrnhut where he was strengthened in his

spiritual life. He also saw among them principles and details of organisation which he afterwards used. William Carey, the Father of Modern Missions, owed much of his inspiration to the Moravians. It was the exploits of the Moravians that awakened missionary zeal in Robert Moffatt. The first missionaries of the London Missionary Society went forth with Moravian instructions in their pockets.

To these people the world is largely indebted for the great evangelical revival and the modern world-wide missionary movement.

WILLIAM CAREY

In 1792 William Carey preached his famous sermon, "Expect Great Things from God, and Attempt Great Things for God." He was then a penniless cobbler-pastor, obscure to the world, with a wife and a young growing family. God had called him to the mission field, and the burden of the heathen so possessed him, that in spite of tremendous difficulties he founded the Baptist Foreign Missionary Society and accomplished a work in India that inspired the whole Christian church with a world vision.

Ernie caught the vision and decided to launch into a new missionary venture.

In 1960 I began to hear and read of great gospel campaigns being carried on in different parts of the world. These crusades were simply known as, "Every Home Crusades." They were already operating in over one hundred countries under the leadership of Dr. Jack McAllister. As the title suggests, every home in a country, or a certain area, was being reached with the gospel message by means of the printed page.

I was very impressed to read that Tokyo, one of the largest cities in the world, had been reached twice over with the gospel through the work of the Every Home Crusade in Japan.

As I pondered the question What is an Every Home Crusade? I was drawn to Acts 5:42, "And daily in the temple, and in every house, they ceased not to teach and preach Jesus Christ." Again in Acts 20:20; "I... have taught you publicly, and from house to house." The early Christians took the "every creature" command of the Lord Jesus literally, and we should do the same. Every home evangelism is a systematic effort to place a clear cut gospel message and invitation, in every home in a country.

One evening I was in a large conference meeting at Kiladeas, near Enniskillen. Dr. Oswald J. Smith of Toronto was speaking about this ministry. He said, "Do you know that you owe everything you are as a Christian to the printed page? Had it not been for the Word of God, you would not have been a Christian. The Bible says, 'faith cometh by hearing, and hearing by the Word of God.' What was it that gave us the Reformation? You may think it was Martin Luther's preaching; I do not believe it was. Martin Luther translated the New Testament and later the Old Testament into the German language, and through the reading of the Scriptures and the preaching of the Gospel the glorious Reformation took place. I know of no other way by which we can carry out our Lord's command, apart from the printed page. The Bible says the gospel must first be published among all nations. Well then, let us publish it. Let us put out simple gospel messages filled with Scripture, and let us circulate them far and wide."

"Church buildings or the gospel message?" Oswald Smith continued. "We have been putting too much of our money into buildings, instead of into the message. That is where the Christian church has made a great mistake. It is the gospel message that is dynamite. It is the gospel that is the power of God unto salvation, not the building but the gospel message."

In that meeting the Lord seemed to be calling me to go forward to commence such a ministry in Northern Ireland. In obedience to what I believed to be His will, I began to prepare a gospel leaflet called "Good News", to be used in this campaign. The leaflet contained a clear gospel message, and at the end of the leaflet we placed a special invitation in the following words:

"If you desire to know the Lord Jesus Christ as your Saviour, please send us your name and address in block capitals, and we will send you a free copy of the booklet 'Pardon for Sin and Assurance of Peace With God' by W. J. Patton.

Send to:
Mr. William E. Allen,
Every Home Crusade,
43 Oakland Avenue,
Belfast, BT4 3BW,
Northern Ireland"

I also began to prepare the booklet for persons who would desire to know the way of salvation. This booklet was called "Pardon for Sin and Assurance of Peace with God" and was composed of portions from the book called Pardon and Assurance which was written by W. J. Patton of Dromara, Co Down, Northern Ireland. Mr. Patton was a minister of the Gospel who was mightily used of God. Through his preaching and writings, multitudes of souls were won to our Lord Jesus Christ. He, being dead, is still speaking. Since this booklet was first published we have printed millions of copies in booklet and leaflet form in different languages.

In addition we also prepared a Bible reading guide, which enables a person to read through the whole Bible in one year. We planned that we would send a personal letter explaining the way of salvation through the Lord Jesus Christ to every person who wrote to us. We also planned to send each of these enquirers a free copy of "Pardon for Sin and Assurance of Peace with God" and a copy of the Bible reading guide.

This expansion of their ministry made it impossible for Ernie and Kathleen to continue working with the church in East Belfast.

It was with a sad heart that he left this congregation. The couple bade farewell to the pastoral ministry of the local church as the Lord opened the door into another ministry that would touch and bless thousands of churches all over the world. God had called, and His children must follow.

In the May-August edition of the Revival Movement's magazine in 1960 Ernie gave announcement of the new emphasis and thrust of the work.

> Every Home Crusade is the name of a new branch of our witness which is now being formed - a crusade aiming to place a clear gospel message and invitation in every home in Northern Ireland and praying that this kind of witness may be extended throughout the British Isles.
>
> A new large gospel pamphlet, printed in two colours and illustrated with clear, but Scriptural messages, has been published, and its circulation has already begun. We have in our country about 200,000 homes, and if local Christians will join in this effort, then every home could be reached within a few years. When Jesus fed the multitudes, He had them sit in fifties, and in hundreds so that each one would be fed. He had this work done systematically. How much more important it is to share around the gospel of our Lord Jesus Christ systematically. He is the Bread of Life, and He is the only Saviour of men.
>
> We ask you to pray for this Crusade for souls. Will you ask the Lord what He will have you to do for those in the villages and towns, not only of Ireland, but throughout the British Isles?

In the same edition of the magazine Ernie printed a powerful challenge written by Dr. Oswald J. Smith.

> For the first time in six thousand years people in large numbers are learning to read. No less than a million

people every seven days learn to read for the first time. Now what are they going to read? Of course they will read anything they can get their hands on. They are hungry for literature.

Do you know what you would see if you were to visit the Asiatic world and look at the book-stands? You would see beautifully coloured magazines. They are the magazines of the Communists. The Communist presses are going day and night, and they are turning out tonnes upon tonnes of literature. Very little of it is being sent to the western world. Most of it goes to Africa and the different Asiatic countries.

Why, they even claim that they won China by the printed page. Now they want to win the whole world. Do you know how many pieces of literature the Communists printed in one year? The Communists printed, within just one year two pieces of literature for every man, every woman, every boy and every girl on the face of the earth. The Communists are on the job.

Five hundred magazines per minute. What else will you see on the bookstands? You will see another series of beautifully printed magazines. They are put out by Jehovah's Witnesses. Do you realize that Jehovah's Witnesses have one press which is the largest religious press in the world, and that it runs day and night? It prints no less than 500 magazines per minute. That means 84,000,000 magazines a year. They are sent to the Asiatic world, to Africa and to many other countries. They are going to win them to their cult if at all possible.

Now, to a large extent, they are succeeding. They are baptising hundreds while we are baptising twos and threes. And every convert has been won by means of the printed page. They do not build expensive churches. They put their money where it will count most. They put it into the printed page, into the message. They send their message out to those who do not have it in an effort to reach them.

£5,000,000 for the printed page. Do you know how much money the Seventh Day Adventists put aside in one year for the printed page? They set aside over £5,000,000. How much has your denomination set aside? The Seventh Day Adventists know something of the power of the printed page, and they are determined to get their message out.

"Reaching Every Creature." I know of no other way by which we can carry out our Lord's command to reach every creature, apart from the printed page. I know of no method to compare with the printed page. It is needed on every field. The Bible says the gospel must first be published among all nations. Well, then, let us publish it. Let us put out simple salvation messages, filled with Scripture, and let us circulate them far and wide. Why then waste God's money? Why not put it where it will count most? Why not invest it in the printed page?

Why the printed page is so effective?

It is the easiest way to approach a sinner.
It needs no public meeting place and can go anywhere.
It is always faithful and can speak on any subject.
It is not overcome by fear, opposition or weariness.
It can be studied in secret and receive undivided attention.
It is backed by the prayers of the distributor.
It remains to minister to hearts over and over again.

Chapter Six

HIGHWAYS AND BYWAYS

God never puts a man in any place that is too small for him to grow. When Ernie first published the "Revival Series" booklets it was not his intention to develop a literature ministry. His emphasis had been on the subject of revival rather than the actual literature that he produced. However, the surrendered life can be led into paths that usher one into open plains of service where they engage in greater things for the Lord. Out of the Revival Movement that Ernie founded, Every Home Crusade developed. This new endeavour became part of the Revival Movement Association, an umbrella name for all the various aspects of Ernie's ministry.

The Allen's house on Omeath Street which was already full was soon bursting at the seams, full of leaflets, booklets and books. It became evident that the family would have to move. Ernie and Kathleen prayed about this, and the Lord opened the way to procure a larger house in Oakland Avenue, off the Upper Newtownards Road in East Belfast.

Ernie shared with supporters and friends what he felt God had put on his heart. Soon others caught the enthusiasm and vision for this work. Ernie recalls:

> To commence Every Home Crusade in Northern Ireland, we began to plan to reach every home in County Fermanagh with the gospel leaflet, "Good News." In order to do this we bought the electoral list for the whole county from the council offices in Enniskillen. At that time I had the help of a very good typist, and we paid the post office vans to deliver the literature to all the homes in the country districts.
>
> In February 1962, a number of keen young Christian men who heard about our venture came forward to help in this every home crusade. The leader of this group was the late George Hamilton, and he was ably assisted by Ernie McKeown, Arthur Darragh and other friends. (Arthur Darragh's mother had supported the "Revival Movement" since 1952, and Arthur caught the enthusiasm of his mother.)
>
> These friends held open air meetings and distributed the leaflets to all the homes in Enniskillen. They then started to visit all the towns and villages of County Fermanagh which included Lisnaskea, Newtownbutler, Maguiresbridge, Belcoo, Irvinestown, Rosslea, Magheralave, Lisbellaw, Tempo, Garrison and Belleek. All of this work was bathed in prayer. It took one year to reach every home in County Fermanagh.
>
> After the literature witness to every home in County Fermanagh was completed, attention focused on County Tyrone, which had a population then of about 133,000. Again the electoral lists of all the county were obtained, and the workers began to mail the gospel leaflet "Good News" to every home in the country districts.
>
> Another group of fine young Christian men embarked on a mission to place the gospel literature in every home in all

the towns and villages of County Tyrone. Within a few months they visited the following towns and villages; Cookstown, Dungannon, Coalisland, Moy, Moygashel, Stewartstown, Donaghey, Tullyhogue, Fivemiletown, Aughnacloy, Strabane, Moneymore, Magherafelt, Castledawson, Maghera, Tobermore, Desertmartin, Draperstown, Swatragh, Kilrea, Garvagh, Bellaghy, and Curran.

When the witness in County Tyrone was completed, attention then turned to County Londonderry. In November 1964, systematic visitation was commenced to reach every home in the large city of Londonderry with its population of 53,000 people. At the same time teams engaged in reaching the homes in the rural and mountain districts of the county.

One of the workers reported that during the visitation in a country area he had given a ride to a Roman Catholic lady and her two sons. He had witnessed to them of the Lord Jesus Christ as the only Saviour, and had given to the woman a copy of the booklet, "Pardon for Sin, and Assurance of Peace with God".

A few months later, he was in the same town, and a woman spoke to him, "Sir, do you not know me? You are the gentleman who gave me the booklet called 'Pardon for Sin, and Assurance of Peace with God.'"

"Yes," he said, "I remember now."

"Well," she said, "I wanted to tell you how much I enjoyed reading it. I have read it over and over again."

The worker asked her, "Have you done what the booklet told you to do? Did you trust the Lord Jesus Christ as your personal Saviour?"

The lady replied, "I did not know that I could do that."

He explained to her how to accept the Lord Jesus, and asked her, "If you do this, do you believe He will forgive your sins and be your Saviour?"

She replied, "Yes, I believe He will."

The soul-winner further pressed, "Do you believe that He will save you now?"

To this the woman replied, "Yes, I do."

Standing together on the footpath of the town's public thoroughfare, they prayed together. This Roman Catholic woman prayed aloud and trusted the Lord Jesus Christ as her personal Saviour.

During the widespread distribution of the gospel leaflets in Fermanagh, Tyrone and Londonderry, Ernie and his friends also engaged in many other evangelistic outreaches. Some looked for bereavement notices in local newspapers and wrote to many grieving families to express sympathy. With the letter they would enclose appropriate gospel tracts. Another willing company of workers showed interest in distributing gospel tracts.

George Walmsley became involved in this ministry and distributed Every Home Crusade tracts on the busy streets of Belfast every week. He often visited parts of the city that were considered by some to be "no go" areas. He made such an impact on the Falls Road, a mainly Roman Catholic part of Belfast, that his testimony was printed in the local tabloid, The Andersontown News.

Every Sunday for fifteen years Mr. & Mrs. Robert McKnight distributed Every Home Crusade literature to all the patients at the Lagan Valley Hospital in Lisburn. This was a ministry of encouragement to those who were sick.

Miss Gladys Blackburne, a retired school teacher, was a remarkable lady. She had a special burden for the security forces and had a good relationship with the British Army. For over twenty years she personally met every soldier who arrived in Ulster and gave each one a stamped envelope and writing paper to write home, a bar of chocolate and an Every Home Crusade gospel tract. On one occasion she travelled up country to visit a particular group of soldiers in a certain barrack. She was having such a good time encouraging some of the young recruits that when she realised the time she found she had missed the last bus home to Belfast. Word of her predicament reached the Commander, and he ordered an army helicopter to transport the marooned lady home. On another occasion Miss Blackburne was made aware that there was to be a meeting of the Army Council of the Provisional Irish Republican Army. She was to have an appointment at noon, but she abandoned her plans and hurried to the location to meet the IRA men emerging from their council meeting and placed an envelope containing gospel tracts in the hand of each one.

Ernie also prayed about placing advertisements with gospel messages into newspapers right across the country. The Lord supplied the funds to make this idea a reality, so Ernie got busy. He placed the advertisements in a wide variety of newspapers from Belfast to Enniskillen and from Newry to Londonderry. They read:

The World's Next Great Event

We are all standing upon the threshold of an awe-inspiring future. The next great event in world history will be the coming again of our Lord Jesus Christ for His people. The Lord Himself shall descend from Heaven with a shout, with the voice of the Archangel and with the trump of God. And the dead in Christ shall rise first. Then we which are alive shall be caught up together with them in the clouds to meet the Lord in the air.

Jesus foretold the resurrection of His people. He said, "I am the Resurrection and the Life. There was a pleasant little family in Bethany which Jesus loved, Martha, Mary and Lazarus. Lazarus died and was buried in a cave. Jesus cried with a voice, which will one day thunder through the vast charnel-house of the dead and bid all His people live, "Lazarus, come forth," and Lazarus came forth alive.

With what body do they rise? The same body which dies. It is sown in corruption. It is sown in dishonour; it is raised in glory. It is sown a natural body, it is raised a spiritual body. How are the dead raised up? St. Paul answers. God's power is pledged to perform this. That power which made the systems of the Universe, that power which carpeted this planet with emerald, roofed it with azure and lit it up with ten thousand suns that power is pledged to raise me from the dead.

On that day the trump of God shall sound and thunder through death's vast empire. Old abbeys, cathedrals and caverns will be vocal with life. From the battlefields of the world they will come. And all the saved from all around the world will hail redemption's grand consummation.

Jesus is coming soon! Are you ready for this great event? If you are concerned about this subject, write to us and we will send you a free copy of the booklet, "Pardon for Sin and Assurance of Peace with God" by W. J. Patton. Christian friend, send for a free copy of the booklet "Heaven - Home of many Mansions". Write to:

Mr. W. E. Allen
EVERY HOME CRUSADE
43 Oakland Avenue,
Belfast 4,
N. Ireland

There was a good response to this witness that reached into many homes. One young man wrote:

Dear Mr. Allen,

I saw your name in the Gospel message in the Impartial Reporter last Friday night. I am all alone in the world since the sudden death of my mother. I have had no peace of mind since my mother's death after she spent only three days in hospital. Her sudden end made me think of myself. I would like to have peace of mind and to know the Lord Jesus Christ as my Saviour. When I saw your name I made up my mind to write to you. Please send me the booklet "Pardon for Sin, and Assurance of Peace with God."

Such was the demand for copies of the booklet "Pardon for Sin, and Assurance of Peace with God," that by the beginning of 1965, 20,000 copies of this booklet had been printed.

Door-to-door visitation can at times be risky in what may be considered to be "inhospitable districts." Mr. Tom Mann and Mr. Robert Dain, wearing gospel jackets and supplied with thousands of Every Home Crusade tracts, carried the witness of the gospel to Crossmaglen, Dungiven, the Bogside and to the Tantalus and Creggan housing estates. They saturated this outreach in prayer and trusted God for His protection. They also travelled to the Catholic areas of Armagh, Londonderry, Strabane and Belfast. They also conducted an evangelistic tour of Wales during which they distributed tens of thousands of gospel leaflets. William Moore, William Honeyman and Frank Marshall spent three of their summer months taking the Every Home Crusade literature to many towns in the Republic of Ireland. Such distributors gave legs to the literature printed by the Every Home Crusade, and the goal of reaching out with the gospel into the highways and byways was being accomplished.

Until this juncture in the ministry most of the printing of booklets and leaflets had been done by Ernie's good friends at the Outlook Press in Rathfriland. Ernie prayed about purchasing a press which would enable him to print his own gospel leaflets. The Lord answered his prayers by providing a small printing machine, a Multilith 1250. Once he procured the machine he faced a very practical problem - where to put it? In Ernie's mind there was only one possible place for it - the front living room of their new home. So where most families had a piano for their children's music, the Allens set up a printing press for the work of the Every Home Crusade.

Ernie wrote about this new purchase in the Revival Movement of March 1964: "I am glad to tell you that about three weeks ago we were able to make the full payment for this machine. We are printing on it a new edition of the booklet 'Pardon and Assurance'. Also a new printing of the leaflet 'Jesus the Wonderful'. This week we have a gospel message in two newspapers - The Mourne

Observer and the Armagh Gazette. With the provision of the printing machine the Lord has answered the first part of our prayer for a great new advance towards reaching multitudes all over the British Isles."

By the end of 1965, 576,000 gospel tracts had been printed and distributed for the Every Home Crusade. The circulation of literature was bathed in prayer as people pledged to intercede for this work.

Even with accomplishing so much in so short a time Ernie and Kathleen did not take it as a signal to ease off the volume of work. They pushed and accelerated the witness of the Every Home Crusade with greater gusto. Even in the transportation of literature Ernie made sure the gospel was spread to all they encountered. In order to do this they purchased a van for the use of the Crusade through funds the Lord supplied. The vehicle was appropriately decorated on both sides with gospel slogans: "What must I do to be saved?" "Believe on the Lord Jesus Christ and thou shalt be saved." "Repent ye, and be converted, that your sins may be blotted out through Jesus Christ our Lord." The doors at the rear of the vehicle shared one text on the two panels, "The wages of sin is eternal death; but the gift of God is eternal life."

Groups of young people volunteered days and weeks during their summer holidays to distribute the gospel leaflets. In July 1965, Alec Taylor led such a group of young Christians in placing the Every Home Crusade literature in every home in the towns and villages along the picturesque Antrim Coast Road. They travelled in the Every Home Crusade van displaying the various gospel texts as they travelled between Glenarm and Cushendun visiting Camlough, Waterfoot, Red Bay and Cushendall en route.

During this endeavour a young man on a motor-cycle spotted the gospel van and signalled for them to stop. He engaged Alec Taylor in conversation and told him that he wanted to be saved. The young man had previously gone to a Roman Catholic Chapel to seek spiritual help but had not found what he was looking for. Alec had the joy of leading him to faith in the Lord Jesus Christ.

This enthused and encouraged the group of young people so much that they volunteered to give other days to distributing tracts. Within a period of two weeks they placed literature in every home in Monkstown, Greenisland, Carrickfergus, Whitehead, Ballycastle, Portballintrae and Portstewart.

Other teams began to concentrate their distribution of the literature in Belfast, impartially including both Catholic and Protestant areas. Besides blanketing the towns and villages near to Belfast with the literature, they visited every home in the large housing estates of Dundonald, Derriaghy, Killeaton, Lambeg, Falls Road, Harmony Heights, Culcavey, Long Kesh and Seymour Hill Estate leaving the Every Home Crusade leaflets.

Every day Ernie and Kathleen read and answered correspondence in response to this crusade. This was most encouraging for them. The following is a random selection of excerpts from some of the letters they received.

> "Dear Mr. Allen,
> I am sorry to say that I am not born again. Please pray for me. I am downright in earnest to be saved. Please send me a copy of your booklet 'Pardon for Sin, and Assurance of Peace with God'."

> "Dear Sir,
> Please send me a copy of your booklet 'Pardon and Assurance,' as I desire to know the Lord Jesus Christ as my Saviour."

> "Dear Mr. Allen,
> Please send me one of your booklets, 'Pardon and Assurance.' I would like the Lord Jesus Christ to be my Saviour."

"Dear Sir,

Please send me a free copy of the booklet 'Pardon and Assurance'. I have two small children and would like if you send me some simple tracts that I could read to them."

"Dear Sir,

I do desire to know the Lord Jesus Christ as my Saviour. I am twelve years old. Please send me a copy of your booklet 'Pardon and Assurance'."

"Dear Mr. Allen,

I know that I am saved for eternity, and I never had such happiness before. I attend local meetings, and I find happy fellowship where our Lord's Word is preached. I would like you to send me some gospel tracts, and some of the booklet 'Pardon and Assurance' to give to my neighbours. I have found so much help in this booklet, because it sets the truth out so clearly. I was convicted of my sins and realised that only Jesus could save me. My prayer is with you in winning souls to our Lord Jesus Christ."

One lady wrote out of concern for her own soul, and asked for a copy of the booklet "Pardon and Assurance." Ernie replied to her letter and mentioned that he knew a Christian lady who lived near to where the she lived. He told her that this lady would be glad to pray with her and lead her to the Saviour. Later the lady wrote:

"Dear Mr. Allen,

Please send me the Christian lady's address. I would like very much to see her. I have five sons, and one of them has just been saved. I told him to pray for me."

Many of the souls that were converted as a result of that intensified crusade to place gospel literature in every home are still bearing fruit today. George Whyte, who was raised in the shadow of Slemish Mountain just outside Broughshane in Northern Ireland, was deeply affected through a tract he received from the Every Home Crusade. He is not sure how the small gospel tract from the Every Home Crusade came into his possession, but he remembers that the title simply read, "The Shame of Sin". He gave it a quick read through and admitted mental assent to its message, but George knew that he was a sinner who needed to be saved; however, as a young man he thought he had plenty of time.

George's wife, Rosemary, had already trusted in the Lord Jesus as her Saviour as a result of tent meetings conducted by evangelist Joe Black. She earnestly prayed for her husband, but he continued in his unregenerate ways. Other Christians often spoke to George, but he turned a deaf ear to spiritual matters.

In April 1965, the Michelin Rubber Company where he was employed closed down because of industrial action. Rather than be idle George took a job building for a local farmer, Mr. John McKeown. During that time he was persuaded by his wife to attend a gospel meeting in a local Brethren Hall. On the evening of 15th April 1965 Mr. Tom Wallace preached on the text found in Isaiah 14:9, "Hell from beneath is moved for thee to meet thee at thy coming: it stirreth up the dead for thee, even all the chief ones of the earth..."

George's heart was broken. He returned home after the meeting and picked up the Every Home Crusade tract that he had formerly discarded. As he read "The Shame of Sin" he could not contain the feeling of strong conviction any longer and burst into tears. At 9:20 that same evening he sank to his knees and called upon God for mercy. Rosemary's prayers were answered. God had blessed the gospel tract, and it accomplished its purpose. Another life had been transformed.

Realising he would have to confess his new found faith in Christ to others, George prayed that the Lord would help him show the reality of salvation. While washing up after a hard day's work John McKeown remarked, "George, I see a great change in you today. Has something happened?" George seized the opportunity and immediately confessed that the Lord saved him the previous night. It was the first answer to prayer that George experienced. He was to find out there were many more to follow. George entered the Free Presbyterian Theological Hall in 1976 and was ordained to the ministry in 1980.

Ernie Allen knew nothing of this conversion until George was invited to preach at an Every Home Crusade Conference in Redcar Street many years later. As George related his testimony Ernie was thrilled to learn that this servant of God had been converted through the literature twenty years earlier. Mr. Thompson Eccles, who was in the meeting, wept to hear the testimony, for he had prayed for George Whyte ever since he was orphaned as a young boy. George has been the minister of Coleraine Free Presbyterian Church since 1980 and was instrumental in establishing another Free Presbyterian outreach congregation in Bushmills.

Although the printed page was the main thrust of Ernie's ministry, there were also other avenues of service by which he planned to reach the lost with the gospel of the Lord Jesus Christ. Successful evangelistic missions were conducted in Broughshane, Bernagh (near Dungannon), and in the old school house at Castlevennan.

As the ministry of the Crusade developed and the distribution of literature increased the magnitude of the work became too much for Ernie and Kathleen to continue alone. With this heavy on his heart Ernie shared with his supporters that the Lord was asking him to expand the ministry, but more workers would be needed for this great but exacting task. Ernie and Kathleen, motivated by their passion for the lost and for their Lord were completely sold out to this work, and they were seeking coworkers with a similar passion. *Where would they find workers with such a dedication?*

They prayed to the Lord of the harvest to send the labourers for the work.

Chapter Seven

Reaching Up and Stretching Out

An acorn does not become an oak tree over night. The small oak tree not only benefits from the bright sunny days of summer, but also has to endure the cold and harsh days of winter. It grows a little every day through summer and winter. Fierce winds and balmy evenings, deep snow and floods of rain are just some of the rough elements that help make a good oak tree strong.

Just like the tiny acorn God has taken Ernie's life, and since 1938 he has faced many triumphs and challenges. Through these God has allowed him to grow and expand his service for Him. At the outset the quiet and obscure war years at Swansea deepened his roots. The busy and burdened days in which he promoted interest in revival helped to spread his branches. His involvement with people in the pastorate enriched his ministry. Catching the vision for literature evangelism was bearing much fruit. Now was the time for reproduction. This was more than dropping acorns. The time had come to expand the reach of this movement across the world and plant centres of evangelism far beyond the shores of Ulster.

For almost thirteen years the Allens' house acted as a book depot. They lived with books and boxes in almost every room. Literature was Ernie's life. From the first light of morning, Ernie prayed for the tract and booklet ministry. Throughout the day he dispatched parcels and answered correspondence. In the evenings he motivated others and recruited helpers for the cause. At bed time he retired with prayer and thanksgiving on his heart and lips for how the Lord was blessing this growing work.

However, the expanding work required adequate premises to house the literature and provide an office and dispatch room. Again Ernie can look back and see that the Lord was in control, and He was preparing the way for such needs.

> David Ferran who ran a marine business at Belfast Harbour had been a very good friend and a faithful supporter of our work for many years. In the autumn of 1965 he said to me, "Mr. Allen, I would like to invest some money to help your ministry, and the interest on the money would come to you month by month." However, I was not very happy about this proposal.
>
> Up to this time, the work was carried on from our home in Oakland Avenue. Not long before this I had bought a small printing machine and had it placed in our sitting room - my wife was an angel. One day I brought home from the printer 192,000 gospel tracts, 10,000 gospel leaflets and a supply of booklets. There were parcels of literature everywhere in our house.
>
> Eventually I said to my friend, "Brother Ferran, I do not want you to invest money to help this work. What we need is a headquarters; my home is bulging at the seams. We need a store and an office."
>
> "All right," he said, "There is a building for sale at 285 Newtownards Road, I will help you to buy it."
>
> True to his word, in a short time he gave me the money to place a deposit on this building. However, one morning

> not long after David gave me the deposit, the phone rang. Alec Leebody spoke to me and said, "Mr. Allen, I have bad news for you. Your friend David Ferran dropped dead here this morning with a heart attack."
>
> I was stunned at the news of David's sudden death. We had lost a good friend. However, even as I stood there with the phone in my hand, I knew it was the Lord's will to go ahead with the purchasing of this building.
>
> The Lord rallied other supporters around us, and within a short time the needed finance was provided. So quickly did the funds come in that the solicitor said to me, "Mr. Allen, it is not often that a transaction like this is completed so quickly."
>
> The building was just what we needed for the work at that time.

The newly acquired building at 285 Newtownards Road had formerly been a shop. A number of volunteer workers moved in to renovate the building. This refurbishment provided a reception area, an office, a store room and a dispatch room. The new location was primarily designed to be a depot for storing the literature and sending it out, and most of the printing continued to be done by the Outlook Press in Rathfriland. Kathleen was greatly relieved to finally see the printing press, books, booklets and gospel tracts find a new home at the premises the Lord had provided.

As well as providing the building God also provided willing and dedicated workers to manage and run the developing outreach. Billy Glover, a missionary candidate heading for Spain with the Worldwide Evangelization Crusade, while waiting for the Lord to open the door to the Iberian Peninsula, worked at the Crusade's store. Evelyn Sharman came to work as a secretary, and she was followed by Mrs. Best. Billy French had his heart set on reaching children for the Lord in Eastern Europe, but the door opened for him to work at the Every Home Crusade. Morton Coleman, William Sterrit and Billy Carswell provided valuable service in the Crusade store room.

These were only some of the many friends who worked closely alongside Ernie and Kathleen over the next decade in distributing the Every Home Crusade publications.

With the visitation programme to reach homes throughout Northern Ireland well under way the Crusade began to reach out to the rest of the British Isles. Individual Christians and some churches in England, Scotland and Wales responded to the challenge of placing literature in the homes in their towns. Requests for literature kept the small staff in Belfast stretched. They received appeals from many different places for literature to be sent out.

> Glamorgan "Kindly send 1,500 copies of 'Love Lifted Me' for our village."
>
> Edinburgh "Please send tracts for pubs and for door to door visitation."
>
> Skipton, Yorkshire "We have a burden for souls throughout the Yorkshire Dales."
>
> Llanelli "Please send 12,000 tracts for this area."
>
> Paisley, Scotland "Thank you for the tracts. I have been richly blessed."
>
> Llanboidy, Wales "Please send a large quantity of tracts for my locality."
>
> Rhonda Valley "Please send more literature to help reach the homes here."
>
> Witney, Oxford "I have been in tract ministry for four years. I am now full time."

They also continued to get requests from areas of Northern Ireland.

> Bessbrook "Please send a supply of tracts for soldiers in this area."
>
> Sperrin Mountains "Please send 'Pardon and Assurance' for door to door witness."

Pastor John Pennington who lived near Manchester, dedicated most of his time to the public witness of the gospel. Dressed in a gospel jacket, covered with gospel texts, and carrying an umbrella the zealous pastor would visit football grounds, race courses, fair grounds and wherever crowds gathered. At these venues he and his friends distributed thousands of tracts every month. Sometimes they were laughed at and derided, but letters came back to the Every Home Crusade office telling of people who were converted through the gospel literature. One day John reported that his gospel umbrella had been stolen. He asked people to pray for the thief for even inside the umbrella the admonition was given. He told his friends, "Some smart-alec stole my umbrella, but he is in for a surprise for when he opens it he will find it is brandished with the words, 'Be sure your sin will find you out.'"

Reaching across the British Isles with literature was a great leap from the early beginnings of placing literature in homes in Ernie's native Northern Ireland. However, Ernie was not content to stop there. He looked at the map of the world and realised that there were millions of people in distant countries who had never heard, nor read the gospel. He was aware that most of the literature was directed to the people in the British Isles where the gospel was already faithfully preached in many places. His burden grew for the lost who lived in the regions beyond his homeland for whom nothing was prepared and he prayed fervently for them. He asked God to open the door to reach out to the "uttermost parts of the world." God answered that prayer in an amazing way.

Pixie Caldwell was a missionary to Nigeria from Newcastle, Northern Ireland with the Sudan United Mission (now known as Action Partners). When she went there in 1952 she realised there was a great need for Christian literature in that part of the world. On one occasion when she was home due to her father's death she came across a tract among his papers from the Every Home Crusade. That discovery became a very important event in the development of the overseas work of the Crusade. Pixie wrote of the opportunities she was given and how she became burdened for the literature ministry.

A long trail of Fulani tribal people with their cattle suddenly appeared on the horizon. Soon they would disappear. I stopped the car and ran towards them. "Safe journey!" I called, "I have an important message for you about the way to heaven."

"Tell our father. He is behind," replied the young men controlling the cattle. I greeted the women and children, some of whom were borne by the slow moving oxen.

The father came behind the company and asked in Hausa, "Have you any tracts?"

I had only one tract with me that day. As I took it from my handbag he drew out a tiny new plastic bag from his breast pocket, folded the tract carefully and put it inside. A second later he had gone in pursuit of the cattle trail. As I watched them disappear I marvelled that even migrating Fulani had heard of our Christian literature. A tiny plastic bag was ready to protect God's Word. I have no doubt that his heart and the hearts of his family were prepared too.

Many have never heard the gospel in our Nigerian towns and villages. Christian students burdened for others inquired, "Have you any Christian literature for us to distribute during school holidays?" I had just a few tracts. Yet when I prayed about this earnest request from our Nigerian Christian students, God spoke to me very clearly. "Blessed are ye that sow beside all waters." (Isaiah 32:20)

The vision soon became clear - these Christian students could distribute the written Word of God in distant towns and villages, and their witness would be blessed of God.

Although the vision was clear I faced a dilemma. Where could thousands of tracts and literature be obtained? A day or two later, two boxes of tracts were miraculously brought to my home. It was Hudson Taylor who once said, "God's work done in God's way will not lack His supplies."

Soon after that a promise came of a larger and an unending supply of literature from the Every Home Crusade in

Northern Ireland. I had never heard of Every Home Crusade until I found some literature in our Newcastle home in 1965. After my father's home-call I wrote to Mr. Allen about our need in Nigeria but did not have the courage to request thousands of leaflets. He warmly replied to say that he had been looking for an open door in Africa. The Lord wonderfully answered his prayers and ours, and a great door opened.

Through that open door hundreds of thousands of Scripture leaflets, tracts and booklets have entered Nigeria since 1965. Initially all the tracts were in English, but later, tracts and leaflets followed in the Hausa and Fulfulde languages.

The Every Home Crusade also provided literature for the tribal people in Northern Nigeria, Northern Cameroon and the lands bordering the Sahara. This literature has been distributed in churches, schools, hospitals, clinics, market places, by the roadside and in homes. When I worked among the Moslems of the Fulani tribe, I often saw deep joy on their faces as they grasped the written Word of God for the first time. These people knew severe persecution that was exacted on those who witnessed for Christ. The home of one believer who was led to Christ through the literature was burned to the ground.

We praise the Lord for the work of Every Home Crusade and pray for the good Seed sown in the hearts of people in so many lands.

Christ is gathering out a people,
To His name from every race.
Haste to give the invitation,
Ere shall end the day of grace.

The entrance to Africa was the beginning of a ministry that began to spread worldwide. Soon other missionaries were appealing for the gospel tracts and booklets.

Ernie was able to devote more time to preparing other gospel publications with the help of his new co-workers. One publication was "The Way of Salvation made Plain" by R. A. Torrey. He designed and printed a series of "Power leaflets". He transcribed one of W. P. Nicholson's sermons entitled "God's Hell" into tract form. J. C. Ryle's work, "Shall we Know Each Other in Heaven?" went to press and was produced in quantities of thousands. "The Way of the Cross," "Love Lifted Me" and "Eternity - What lies Beyond the Grave?" were also produced. These booklets were produced by the millions. They reached and impacted millions of people worldwide.

The production work of Every Home Crusade increased so greatly that over and above the thousands of booklets which were sent out each week, 100,000 tracts passed through the premises every five days. Over one million tracts were mailed every eight weeks and half of these went to foreign countries. Paper and printing costs for one month in 1974 came to £1,862.58. That was a lot of money then, and the costs of operation were increasing all the time. The income for that year totalled £19,924. They used part of the money to pay for all the general expenses of printing, packaging, postage and running the depot, but ever burdened with the needs of others, they sent a gift of £7,056 to provide Scripture portions for Africans and to help Bible translators in that continent.

In 1973 Ernie reported that the number of people writing to inquire about the way of salvation rose steadily month by month. At the beginning of the year thirty people wrote to the Every Home Crusade in one month. During the next month thirty-three people wrote asking about the way of salvation, and this was followed in the succeeding month by another forty people requesting information about salvation. By the end of that year three hundred and eighty-five people contacted the Crusade's office seeking to know more about salvation through Jesus Christ. This pattern continued each year with multiplying numbers of converts as the capacity of the Crusade increased. This response thrilled and encouraged the hearts of the faithful workers and supporters of the ministry.

Many people gave gifts faithfully and sacrificially to the work. Some sent general gifts for the work. Others expressed interest in purchasing a tonne of paper or paying for a specific bill. Prayer meetings and churches sent gifts which were earmarked for special projects. All these gifts were assuredly investments for eternity.

Appeals for literature began to flood in from an increasing number of countries on all continents. At first fifty requests for literature were received in one month; this rose to twenty-four requests in one day. The need was staggering. Letters came from India, Ethiopia, Uganda, Trinidad, Brazil, Nigeria, Calabar and many other distant countries. One request from the Philippines, requested that 100,000 tracts be sent per month. Another letter asked for 50,000 tracts for the Irish Republic. One Christian brother from Fort Portal, Uganda, East Africa wrote the following letter.

> Dear Mr. Allen and Friends,
>
> I am an overseer of seventeen churches. Yesterday I returned from a visit to all our churches to encourage them in the Lord. I found them lacking gospel literature. I saw six men fighting for a single gospel tract. When I saw this, I fell down on my knees and asked the Lord to help us and to make a way for us to have the Scriptures and the literature which we need.
>
> You have been a blessing to us by sending us your gospel tracts and leaflets. One Pastor told me that six persons, after reading the gospel tracts, had come to him in tears asking to be prayed with, and they received Jesus as their Lord and Saviour. Ten students in a school accepted the Lord Jesus as Saviour, after one of our young people had distributed tracts to the whole school.
>
> The whole staff of Bukhalika Primary School and many of the children came to Christ after they heard the message in one of the tracts preached to them. I saw teachers crying with conviction of sin and students alike. One woman who

was a well known witch doctor came to Christ after hearing the gospel message.

Brethren, your literature is a great help to us. Thank you for the great love you have shown to us. Our great problem is that we have no Bibles. Most of our members do not have Bibles. Please send us two thousand Bibles and many more boxes of tracts and leaflets. May God bless you in abundance.

From Pastor Chris Kallusa.

Ernie and his friends endeavoured to attend to all these appeals. The printing, packaging and postage of this literature was accomplished at the expense of the Every Home Crusade and sent free of charge to those who needed it overseas. God honoured these steps of faith.

Each year thousands of letters arrived reporting hundreds of conversions as a result of the literature distributed in numerous countries. The results were astounding, and although the reading of letter after letter may seem somewhat repetitive and tedious the workers at the Every Home Crusade recognised the magnitude of this work as almost incomprehensible. Pastors, evangelists and lay workers were giving feet to the literature and taking it to isolated regions. This brought about the conversion of many people. One man wrote from Nigeria and said, "You have reduced the population of hell by a million." Only an infinite God could use printed paper to do such an outstanding work.

In 1975 Ernie and friends stretched themselves further and designed cartoon posters which highlighted the evils of alcohol and gambling and displayed the only way of deliverance as through the Lord Jesus Christ. These became very popular, and packages were sent to many countries.

In 1976 the Crusade started to print hundreds of thousands of large gospel posters which found their way around the globe. Gospel calendars soon followed, and these were displayed in all sorts of places and had a great effect. During December 1977, seven hundred and eighty-seven people wrote from different parts of the world, registering their decision to receive Jesus Christ as Saviour.

Every Home Crusade took yet another step forward which not only widened their influence but also pointed the way for the future development of their ministry. Dr. Kurien, the President of the All India Prayer Fellowship wrote and challenged Ernie.

> Dear Brother Allen,
>
> We are printing all the tracts which you sent us. One hundred thousand copies have already been printed. I am sending you two copies of the booklet, "Pardon and Assurance" in the Kannada language. This booklet is now being printed in several languages.

Until this stage Every Home Crusade had published all of its literature in English, and it was sent from the headquarters in Belfast to various destinations abroad. In India Christians caught the vision to print the literature they received in their own country but first had to translate the literature into various languages. Several months later Dr. Kurien wrote again:

> Dear Brother Allen,
>
> We are trying our best to print one million tracts a month. Pray that this may be done. We offer the booklet "Pardon and Assurance" and a free Bible course to all who seek to be saved. Please send us five hundred of these booklets per month. Pray for the great work in India. We have one hundred and seventy-one full-time workers, and we publish the literature in seventy-five languages.

Soon word came from Finland to say that over one hundred thousand copies of "Pardon and Assurance" had been published in the Finnish language. Ernie ensured that every year a large percentage of the money that the Crusade received as gifts was channelled beyond the immediate work in Belfast and sent to aid Bible translators who were reaching many tribal groups in multiple languages.

If the Lord wanted the Every Home Crusade to print in foreign languages who could spearhead that work?

PHOTOGRAPHS

Ernie Allen in Bible College 1940

Several Tonnes of Paper being unloaded by hand at the Redcar Street Factory.

The Opening and Dedication of the Building in Redcar Street March 1979

Ernie Allen beside a supply of paper at the Outlook Press in Rathfriland. Below : A Consignment of Literature packed into Tea Chests for Diguna Mission in Kenya which has just been loaded in Redcar Street.

Frederick Starrett who operated this folding machine until his brutal murder in 25th February 1988.

Pastor John Pennington and some of his friends witnessing and distributing our Gospel Tracts in England.

Souls seeking the Saviour during an Evangelistic campaign in Nigeria.

Some of the 8,000 people who attend the Services in "The New Creature Evangelical Church", in Lagos, Nigeria. Some of the hundreds of 5Kg Parcels of Literature which have been sent to Nigeria for distribution to Pastors, Evangelists and Churches throughout this Nation of 100,000,000 Souls.

Some of the 700 friends who attended the opening of the new Literature Factory in Clara Street, Belfast. 1991

Paul Roberts who operates this Heidelberg 102ZP which prints millions of copies of the Gospel of John. Below : Pastors each collecting a 5Kg Parcel of Gospel literature in Ghana.

Prisoners engaged in prayer in a prison in Brazil.

20 Tonnes of Paper being unloaded at the factory

A Diguna Mission Evangelistic Team and Choir beside one of their lorries. Below : A Church Service in Kisangani, Zaire where our literature was distributed after the Service. (See the back cover)

Chapter Eight

Where Are The Workers?

A humorous person wittingly once commented, "The only man who ever got all his work done by Friday was Robinson Crusoe." There was certainly no "Man Friday" at the Every Home Crusade literature depot. All of the team were fully committed to the work and fully stretched to the limit at their particular jobs. At times the increasing challenge and expanding opportunities opening up for the Every Home Crusade not only overwhelmed the small team but made them realise they required some specialist workers. This need was made a definite focus of prayer. The need was particular because not only did they require men who were specialist within their field, but they would have to have men of uncommon dedication and have complete confidence in the aim of the Every Home Crusade - taking the gospel to every creature. God had already his men chosen for the task, and they were even closer than Ernie Allen could have imagined.

The Allen family was closely knit. Ernie and Kathleen had one daughter, Heather, and twin sons, Paul and Clive. These children were reared under the godly influence of a mother and father who were totally sold out to the Lord and His work. Even as children, their parents example and zeal made a deep impression in their young lives. While Ernie had the joy of leading many people to the Lord in various meetings, nothing gave him more delight than to lead his own children to personal faith in Jesus Christ.

Paul was converted when he was only eight years old. As he was getting ready for bed one evening, he expressed to his father that he would like to ask the Lord Jesus into his heart. Father and son knelt together, and Paul prayed the sinner's prayer and accepted Jesus as his Saviour. As he grew older he maintained a Christian witness at school. Inevitably he found that some of his spare time was taken up helping his dad in the front room of their Oakland Avenue home, either filling envelopes or folding leaflets.

When the Every Home Crusade moved to the Newtownards Road, Paul and Clive often spent their summer holidays packing boxes and helping where needed at the literature depot. However, they relished a welcome respite from Belfast when they made summer visits to Kathleen's family in Portavogie where they enjoyed trips on the fishing boats.

From high school Paul gained an entrance to the Belfast College of Business Studies. There he prepared for whatever God had in store. After completing his studies, he wrestled with what God would have him do. Should he follow a career in the secular world or was the Lord opening a door into Christian work? He did not want to follow his father into the work of the Every Home Crusade without knowing it was God's will for his life. After some time of prayer and consultation Paul took the step of faith and became a full-time worker with the Crusade in May, 1978. This made his father very happy.

Paul did not step into any particular role. Like everyone else involved, he was ready to help in any department. As the work grew and developed, he assumed the book-keeping responsibilities from his mother and much of the clerical work. Correspondence alone was a demanding job. On one day, two hundred thirty-three letters arrived from various countries. They contained appeals for literature, news of conversions, gifts for the ministry and letters of thanks. On another day five hundred and three letters were received; two hundred of these were from people inquiring about the way of salvation.

On one occasion due to a mail strike, incoming foreign correspondence dried up for more than a month. Six thousand letters arrived in one day when it was over. Every person in every department was snowed under with work as a result. Letters needed to be answered, and the printing and packaging staff had to try to keep up in order to meet the appeals made for literature.

The good harmony that exists among the work force at the Crusade is unusual. Compatibility and unity in the work place is important, yet when nineteen workers rub shoulders with each other for eight hours every day, there is the potential for discord and strife. These workers are not robots, nor are they alien to stress. They may have different opinions about certain matters. Paul can testify that the devotional time together at the beginning of each day enhances good fellowship throughout the factory, and undoubtedly this is the secret of their excellent production levels.

Paul views his work like it is a cog in the over all machinery of the printing factory. Each person has to do his job in order for everything else to function properly. Paul is responsible for paying the bills, assessing and paying the wages, satisfying the Inland Revenue and completing the general book-keeping. It is remarkable to see how God provides in this area, and Paul is amazed at how good God has been to them. Every Home Crusade is a non-profit making organisation and is a registered charity. Their literature is sent abroad free of charge to Christian workers who use it among their people; therefore, the Crusade has no guarantee of income other than to stand on the promises that God has given them. For over sixty years Ernie Allen has proved that these promises are totally dependable. Day by day, week in and week out, supporters faithfully send their gifts to sustain this work.

Right from the beginning when Ernie Allen founded the Revival Movement, and subsequently the Every Home Crusade, he firmly believed in the principle of faith. That was how he lived, and he felt that is how God's work should be conducted. Ernie believed that the Revival Movement should not incur debts nor take financial risks. Their sole assets were the tools they used. Their sole investments were measured in eternity. Purchases were made only when money was available. These basic principles have never failed; God's promises cannot fail, and the work continues to grow.

The increasing worldwide appeal for literature constantly challenges the Every Home Crusade to stretch to meet greater limits of production. Every step they take to increase their output is matched by the generosity of their supporters. Undoubtedly, it is the Lord who ultimately balances the accounts. Paul finds it fascinating to watch the income from donors transformed into paper, printed and then shipped around the world. It makes him realise that the God who sent ravens to feed Elijah still works miracles today.

It has been said that work without vision is a drudgery, vision without work is mere dreaming, but when vision and work are welded together, it makes that person a missionary. Ernie Allen was a man of vision. For him the literature ministry is much more than a storage and dispatch depot. It seemed that every week he had a vision of their potential and the possibility of the Every Home Crusade outgrowing its current limited capacity. However, Ernie was not one to sit and wait for things to happen. He was pro-active. He prayed that God would send him the right men for this work and then went out and recruited them.

During deputation meetings Ernie made periodic visits to Ballymacbrennan Prayer Union Hall near Lisburn. He had been struck by the sincerity of a young man there who seemed destined for Christian work. Samuel Adams was raised in a Christian home, and like the Allen twins, had been greatly influenced by his godly parents. His father was the leader of the Ballymacbrennan Prayer Union. However, it was literature that fittingly played a major part in young Samuel's conversion to Jesus Christ.

Church attendance on Sunday was part of the Adams' family life. Even though the seven year old boy tried to listen to the minister preach, it was not the persuasive discourse from the pulpit that brought Samuel to faith in Jesus Christ. Instead, Samuel was attracted by the colourful pictures on a large story book. He began to leaf through the pages that told and illustrated the life of the Saviour. When he got to the scene of the Lord Jesus dying on Calvary's cross it forcefully struck him that Jesus Christ died for him. He called his mother, and after a few simple questions Samuel and his mother knelt down together. With child-like simplicity, he asked God to forgive his sins and asked the Lord Jesus to be his Saviour. That important step, precipitated by the pages of a children's book, not only shaped his life but was a veiled pointer to Samuel's future involvement with Christian literature.

After completing his "A Level" exams Samuel who had been raised on a farm, set his sights on university to study horticulture. He loved the farm and the outdoor life. However, he made his future career a matter of prayer and laid his heart open for God to direct him. The Lord soon redirected his attention to a different kind of sowing which involved a more productive Seed that would yield a better harvest. God answered Samuel's prayers in an unmistakable manner.

While Samuel was attending a Child Evangelism Fellowship Missionary Rally in Lisburn, God spoke to his heart. The challenge of a full-time Christian vocation loomed before him. The young man was perplexed. He wanted God's will but was afraid of insidiously being sucked into conforming to other people's opinions. He earnestly prayed that if it were not the Lord's voice, then the persisting sentiment would leave him. He discovered that the opposite happened. The challenge was more than a sentiment, it was a growing conviction that God had a plan for his life.

He shared his feelings with other Christians and enquired about Bible College and possible training for Christian service. Friends advised that because of his youth and inexperience, he should take a job for a year. Edward Douglas, general manager of the Faith

Mission Bookshops, was a close friend of the family, and he recognised the potential of the young man and invited him to work at the Faith Mission Bookshop in central Belfast.

Samuel accepted the position and felt right at home among the books at the Faith Mission. He stacked shelves, priced stock, prepared orders, sold to the public and got to know the best authors. He became familiar with all the books and stock.

One day while he put the price tag on one penny bookmarks, he questioned in his own mind if working in a bookstore was what the Lord had for him. The answer soon came when Samuel found reassurances from God's Word, "He that is faithful in that which is least, is faithful also in much." So satisfying and fulfilling was the work at the Faith Mission that instead of one year at the bookshop, Samuel stayed on for three years. Edward Douglas was delighted that he had found such a good worker.

Just when it seemed that Samuel had found a permanent niche in the bookshop, a change of direction came as a surprise for Samuel and as a disappointment to his friends he worked with at the Faith Mission. He experienced unsettled feelings in his heart about long term commitment to the bookstore. He tried to banish the thoughts, but as he knelt to pray and when he read the Scriptures, the feelings persisted. Just as he had previously experienced the Lord's guidance which brought him to the Faith Mission, he confidently asked the Lord to either remove the restless thoughts or to open a new door.

One week later he received a phone call from Ernie Allen. Samuel was familiar with the growing literature ministry of Every Home Crusade and often prayed for that work. When Ernie explained his vision for the work, he extended an invitation to Samuel to consider joining the Every Home Crusade team. The young man was overwhelmed in one sense, and yet not surprised at God's perfect timing. He knew the Lord was in control of this matter.

Correspondingly, before Ernie spoke to Samuel, he was praying about workers for the expansion of the Crusade, and his mind had been drawn to Samuel. As Ernie contemplated this he was reluctant to approach the young man for he felt he was already committed to the Faith Mission and was unlikely to leave it to work in a print shop. For nearly three weeks Ernie prayed about the matter, and then he decided to test the waters and approach Samuel. God was at work in both cases at the same time and made the transition dovetail.

Mr. Douglas was on holiday when Ernie gave the invitation to Samuel to consider joining the Crusade. Samuel felt the Lord was in these happenings immediately when Ernie made the suggestion, yet he did not make any decision in haste. After due consideration and waiting on the Lord, Samuel arrived at the conclusion that this was the Lord's direction for his life. Peace flooded his heart even though his decision to leave the bookshop was a disappointment to his colleagues. Edward said to Mr. Allen, "You have taken away my right arm."

When Samuel arrived at 285 Newtownards Road in August 1978, he knew why God had given him many Bible promises while he was waiting on the Lord. Without them he would not have survived. The Every Home Crusade needed £100 per day to meet its operational demands. They did not sell any material to raise funds. This was a big step of faith. Although Samuel was ready for anything, he had never seen a printing press in his life. He had to learn quickly, for he was thrown in at the deep end of the printing world.

The purchase of a new printing press at a cost of £5,250 coincided with Samuel's arrival at the Every Home Crusade depot. It was an ideal time for the newcomer to start. The new Multilith 1850 replaced the old machine that had been transferred to the depot from Ernie's Oakland Avenue home. With the purchase of the machine, a three day orientation course was offered to learn how to operate it. That three day course was Samuel's brief initiation.

Very soon he mastered the necessary skills to gain maximum benefit from the Multilith. The new machine was revolutionary for work of the Crusade. It was able to print 6,000 sheets per hour which were then guillotined into 24,000 tracts or 48,000 leaflets.

Samuel was kept busy. Even though he was part of the team, he was located away from his colleagues at the rear of the renovated shop. This isolation, added to by his use of ear muffs to lessen the noise and protect his ear drums, made life lonely and the days long. At first he found the solitude of his new job difficult to deal with after so much interaction with people at the book shop. However, he soon found he was able to turn those lonely hours into profitable and enjoyable times of communion with His Lord.

Samuel was amazed at the reports which arrived daily from around the world. The requests for literature seemed endless. With such demands the depot stayed busy. Tonnes of paper were purchased for tracts. Thousands of booklets arrived from the Outlook Press. Hundreds of packets were sent through the post office. In the early days, nearly all the overseas packets were mailed and the largest parcels weighed no more than five kilos. It became apparent that this growing operation would soon need larger premises and more help.

Clive Allen was Paul's twin. Like Paul, he was not alien to printing and literature. The whiff of ink and books was common place in their lives. He shared the benefit of a Christian upbringing with Heather and Paul, although he did not always look upon this as a privilege. Even though Clive had been taught the Scriptures during his infant years, conversion did not automatically follow. He can remember that his Dad prayed with him, his brother and sister every morning. On the occasional late morning, these prayer times were held in the car while Ernie drove the children to school. However, Ernie's and Kathleen's prayers for Clive's conversion were not answered until he was fourteen years old.

Ernie had been invited by Miss Finlay to speak at Killinchy Mission Hall outside Newtownards. He took his two boys with him and preached an evangelistic sermon at the Mission Hall. At the conclusion of the service Ernie gave an invitation for any person present to come to Jesus Christ for salvation. One person responded that night. It was young Clive Allen. It was a joy and privilege for Ernie to lead his son to the Saviour and see his prayers answered.

It was not easy for a young teenager to take a stand as a Christian at Annadale Grammar School, the school Clive attended in South Belfast. Clive was greatly helped and encouraged by the Scripture Union which was convened after school hours. At these meetings the young people were taught the importance of finding God's will in their lives.

When it came time to leave school, Clive's involvement in his father's literature work helped shape his own decision to follow a career in printing. Like his brother Paul, Clive had also filled envelopes, folded leaflets and ran errands for the Every Home Crusade throughout his boyhood years. Clive love the summer months when he could spend time beside the sea at Portavogie. His Grandad was a fisherman, and nothing gave Clive and his brother more pleasure than a trip on a fishing boat. The fresh air, the steady breezes and a day on the Irish Sea seemed to be everything that a boy would want. Landing a catch was just an added bonus.

These enjoyable school holidays finished when Clive entered into employment as an apprentice letter press printer at Finlay's Packaging Company on Belfast's Ballygomartin Road. There were not many Christians in the print shop, but Clive enjoyed the company and camaraderie of a fine group of fellows. For four and a half years he served his apprenticeship there.

The capacity and output at Every Home Crusade was increasing rapidly, and they desperately needed specialised help. At the back of his mind Clive knew that one day he would join his brother Paul and dad in the literature ministry, and that time had come. Prompted by the pressing need and his father's repeated appeal for workers at the Crusade, Clive resigned from his employment and applied his acquired skills to printing gospel literature at Every Home Crusade.

Although the Crusade had featured greatly in Clive's life, and he loved his job, Clive had a chronic hankering for the sea. He remembered with fondness the fishing boats at Portavogie and the outdoor life on the open seas. For a young man long days at printing machines seemed dull and dismal while the urge for salt water and fishing were in his blood. He finally felt that he had to get it out of his system. Much to everyone's surprise, Clive left the work at Every Home Crusade and went to work on the boats at Portavogie.

This diversion to the fishing boats lasted for one year, during which time he worked with several different crews. Through the family he kept in touch with developments at the Crusade and the print shop and was stirred with the reports of the increasing numbers of people trusting the Saviour. During this time his emotions and sense of priorities seemed to be as tossed and frenzied as the sea waves around him.

Clive continued to be challenged by the drive and dedication of his parents. Besides admiring his father's zeal for the gospel, he greatly respected his mother for the sacrifice she was prepared to make to see his father's goals accomplished. Their example helped him initially decide that the Lord's place for him was with the Every Home Crusade. A short time after he returned to the Crusade's print shop, he attended a meeting where George Bates was preaching. That night at the Branagh Mission in East Belfast, Clive felt constrained to surrender all his life to the Lord Jesus for the work of the Every Home Crusade.

Clive's job is very much on the factory floor supervising the printing presses. Watching machines churn out printed paper may not be everyone's idea of pleasure and satisfaction; however, Clive loves his work. He sees beyond the machine and that through the printed page he is reaching millions of people around the world with the gospel of Jesus Christ. The news of people trusting the Saviour in distant lands through the booklets that roll off his press gives Clive daily inspiration and makes his employment very fulfilling.

Clive agrees with his brother Paul that the secret of good production is found in the sense of unity of aim and purpose in the work force. He is aware that he is not working with a group of angels - his colleagues are young and just as human as he is. They not only share in times of fellowship and prayer, but meal times and coffee breaks often develop into deep theological debates. The men are good friends, and their families often visit with each other, go on holidays together, enjoy picnics in the summer and share the ups and downs of every day life. Even though jokes are shared and pranks are played on each other, in the print area the workers have great respect for the leadership of the Crusade, who provide challenging role models for these young men to follow.

Paul and Clive acknowledge that God worked in their lives, engineering circumstances and bringing about developments for the good of the Crusade, long before they ever thought of it. God also did a work in Heather's life, another unknown blessing that the Lord had prepared for the Allens.

Heather was raised under the same godly influence and impression as her two brothers. She knew the way of salvation since she was an infant. Her parents' prayers were answered when Heather confessed Jesus Christ as her Saviour when she was nine years old. They all attended the Campaigners at Bloomfield Baptist Church, and one summer she went on a campaigner camp to Donaghadee, which is located on the County Down coast almost twenty miles from Belfast. It was a great week of fun with plenty of outdoor activities. Every evening ended with a Bible reading and a devotional talk. After the talk was finished an invitation was given to any young camper to receive the Lord Jesus Christ. Heather made that supreme decision to accept the Lord Jesus as her Saviour after one of the devotional talks. It is something she had wanted to do for so long, and once she did she was glad it was finally settled.

Heather went to school at Bloomfield Collegiate. There she discovered that she not only enjoyed studying French but had an obvious aptitude for languages. This helped set her course for the future. Upon completion of her studies at the Collegiate, Heather enrolled for a bilingual secretarial course which she enjoyed greatly. This led to admission into Queens University, Belfast where she studied German, French and Spanish, and she became proficient and fluent in each.

She also enjoyed visiting her grandparents in Portavogie during the summer vacations. In addition to those summers at the seaside, Heather often joined her brothers in folding tracts, filling envelopes and addressing letters to help mother and father in the Crusade's work. Heather was always impressed with the authenticity and consistency of her parents' dedication to the Lord's work. They lived transparent lives, and all that they professed and preached from the pulpit was outworked as a living reality in the home. It was the example of their practical and faithful Christian lives that moulded Heather's own life and character and helped her depend on the Lord for His guidance.

When Heather chose her university course in languages the Every Home Crusade published their literature only in English and had no plans to branch out into any other language. It wasn't until she was married that the Crusade branched out into the languages in which Heather was fluent.

As a skilled linguist, Ernie's and Kathleen's daughter was ideally suited to handle the foreign correspondence that started to flow into the office. Now married with two children, a boy and a girl, Heather Mercer works from her home and handles all the Spanish, Portuguese and French letters. Although translation can be frustrating at times, and it is difficult to cope with such a volume of mail, Heather is greatly encouraged to press on with her work as she reads of marvellous conversions to Jesus Christ brought about by the medium of the printed page in many countries.

One letter that deeply touched her and impressed upon her the impact of the printed page came from Algeria, a country to which very little literature was ever sent from the Crusade. The author of the letter was a young man who told that he was strolling along a North African beach and came upon a washed up bottle. It contained the Every Home Crusade's "Way of Salvation" booklet in the French language. He had read the booklet and was writing to find out more about the Lord Jesus Christ and the way of salvation.

God provided workers in His own miraculous way, and Ernie was thrilled that his children became part of the work to which he had dedicated his life.

Chapter Nine

On The Move

With the arrival of the new Multilith printing machine more literature was produced, and as a result extra room was urgently needed for storage. Even with the extension that had been done to the building at the Newtownards Road depot, there was still not enough room to house the various aspects of the ever growing work. Ernie foresaw this dilemma and prayed about larger premises. Again the Lord was preparing the way and opening the doors for the work to expand.

The Bible Pattern Church, a small church in Redcar Street located between Belfast's Cregagh and Castlereagh Roads, had functioned in an old converted school building for many years. Sadly their pastor, Pastor Mercer who had been a godly and great man, had died several years earlier, and due to the small numbers the church was considering closure. Ernie heard of this possibility and approached the owner of the building to explore the idea of it being available for the Every Home Crusade to purchase. Ernie was delighted to find that the man was ready to sell.

The building offered adequate space, and it was well proportioned for a print room, a store room and offices. The Crusade had no building fund when Ernie inquired about the premises, but until this juncture the Lord had always supplied their need when He prompted the Crusade to take another step forward. There was no reason to doubt God at this stage.

In September 1978, Ernie sent out an appeal to the supporters of the Crusade in the monthly "Good News" circular.

> Our premises in the Newtownards Road are now much too small for the work. Any of our friends who have called here will verify this fact. We urgently need more space for storage of paper for printing, more room for the stocks of tracts, booklets and leaflets of which we have about one hundred titles in circulation. We also need much more space for our printing department.
>
> With all this in mind we have been looking out for suitable premises for some time. Just now we are considering buying a large property which will be very suitable and would provide us with all the space we so urgently need. To enable us to buy these premises we need £8,000. (The total cost of the property is £16,000.)

In the October prayer letter it was reported that another £2,000 was needed to complete the purchase of the old school building. This amount duly arrived within a short time, and the final payment for the building was made. God honoured their step of faith, and Redcar Street became the new headquarters of the Every Home Crusade in November 1978.

Now that the Crusade had secured the old school building, there was a call for all hands on deck. Renovations had to be made to the building to convert it into a print factory. While the production of booklets and leaflets continued, Mr. Syd Murray, the building contractor, and his team worked hard at knocking down walls, redesigning offices, enlarging the storage area and plastering and painting the building.

On 21st April, 1979, a great congregation of supporters assembled in the refurbished building for an Inauguration Service of Thanksgiving. Pastor Pennington from Manchester and Mr. Bill Wright from Liverpool, who constantly used the Crusade literature at many public venues, came over to Belfast for the occasion. Sydney Murray crowned the full programme of testimony, song and reports with a devotional and challenging message from the Word of God.

Immediately after the opening rally, Alec Leebody used his lorry to help the Crusade transfer the equipment, stock and furnishings from 285 Newtownards Road. It seemed as though the workers in the premises on the Newtownards Road had been suffocated in the old three story shop building with every square foot taken up. Now in Redcar Street they could breathe more freely.

For a while Ernie was able to reserve what had been used as the church sanctuary for conferences, and the other part of the building was converted into a print shop. The former school classrooms were made into a dispatch office, a general office, an office for Mr. Allen and a store.

At the time of transfer from one location to another, the Crusade had only the two Multilith presses and one guillotine. In these new premises there was ample room for more equipment, and that room was needed as the demand for literature grew. In the very week that they moved 1,168 people seeking salvation wrote to the Crusade.

The Crusade's monthly news letter, "Good News," carried a report about the opening of the renovated premises. In that edition they put a few extracts from letters indicating the blessings that the literature was bringing to many souls all over Britain.

A man and his wife saved.

Dear Brother,

I had doubts about my salvation, until I read one of your tracts. Your tracts brought me to the cross of Jesus. They made me realise my sins. My wife and I have received Jesus as our personal Saviour. We have put aside the world and have taken up the cross to follow Jesus. Please send us the booklet, "Pardon and Assurance."

I have been born again.

Dear Sir,

The tracts and leaflets which you sent have been the means through which I have come to know the Lord Jesus Christ as my Saviour. I have been born again in Christ Jesus. I know that He died for me. Please send me tracts for the schools in our town. Thank you, for what you have done for me.

My mind is taken up with the Lord Jesus Christ.

Dear Friends,

I cannot tell you how my mind is taken up with the Lord Jesus Christ, especially when I received Him as my Lord and Saviour. He makes me free from the bondage of sin, and now I am a child of God. One day I was in a quiet place reading John's Gospel chapter three, and I was very astonished at the words.

A converted drunkard wrote from Ayr, Scotland.

Dear Brother Allen,

As a converted drunkard, I feel constrained to tell others, all other drinkers, how they too can be saved. I give a lot of tracts out in our town, and I am saddened to see the great increase in drinking. Please send me three thousand tracts.

A testimony from Exeter.

Thank you for the booklet "Pardon and Assurance." I know that I have complete reconciliation with God through the blood of the Lord Jesus.

In the same monthly letters, the team gave the readers insight to the increasing burdens that rested on the Crusade team.

We have received reports of 1,487 students in seven universities in Nigeria who had professed salvation through the Lord Jesus Christ because of the distribution of the Every Home Crusade tracts in those universities. Most of our literature continues to go to West African countries where a harvest of souls is being reaped for the Lord Jesus Christ. Last month we sent off 280 packets of literature to these countries, and most of these were for students in colleges and schools.

"The Way of the Cross" booklet: We are pleased to receive the reprint of "The Way of the Cross." We are also receiving 13,500 copies of the "Pardon and Assurance" booklet. Hundreds of copies of these booklets are sent out week by week, and many persons write to tell us that they have been led to the Saviour through the reading of these booklets.

Other testimonies were expressed in letters that came from abroad.

A new convert forms a Scripture Union in a school in Ghana.

Dear Teacher,

Thank you for the booklet, "Pardon and Assurance." I now know that Jesus is my Saviour. Teacher, through the help of the Lord I have been able to form a Scripture Union in the secondary school where my father teaches.

From Benin City, Nigeria.

Dear Brother in Christ,

This day I confess myself a guilty sinner. I throw away all my hopes that self-righteousness or church membership or religious ceremonies can save me. From today on I will trust wholly in Jesus Christ. I depend on Him to forgive my sins, to change my heart and to give me everlasting life. I here and now receive Him into my heart and claim Him as my Saviour.

From a young man in Tanzania.

Dear Mr. Allen,

The real life I now have in this body is the result of my trusting in the Son of God who loved me and gave Himself for me. I have been crucified with Christ.

From the International Hospital Christian Fellowship, Holland.

Dear Friends,

Thanks for your excellent publications. We have been using your pamphlet, "Sighs from Hell," by John Bunyan in our training centre, and this has been very revealing to our students. We desire to do the same with a Bible week we are having and also with a new group of students who are starting in September. Please send us fifty more copies.

Good news from Hyderabad, India.

Dear Brother Allen,

We received your parcels with so much literature. In a few days all that you sent in the four boxes was distributed among our evangelists. Do send us bulk supplies. Some evangelists think we should publish your literature in the Telugu language. We can attend to this as we are editing the Telugu edition of the "Herald of His Coming." Please send more revival leaflets too.

An urgent appeal from a team of young evangelists in Nigeria.

Dear Sir,

Having received the experience of full salvation through the blood of our Lord Jesus Christ, and feeling the great burden for lost souls in our area, we the "Gospel Evangelical Team" of young evangelists, apply to you for a supply of heart-searching tracts and for gospel booklets to help new and young Christians to grow in their new life.

Good news of salvation, and an appeal from Ghana.

Dear Friends,

Thank you for the parcels of tracts and leaflets sent to us. Many unsaved souls here were saved through your literature. We are spreading and sowing the seed of the gospel in every direction among unbelievers and pagans. We prayerfully request you again to send us all the tracts you possibly can, and the "Power leaflets".

Two new churches opened in Imo State, Nigeria.

Dear Brethren,

I received your parcels of literature. The Lord is blessing here. He helped us in our two evangelistic campaigns held this year. New churches are now opened in the two places. In the church where I am pastor, souls are being added to the Lord.

A call from Zambia, Central Africa.

Dear Mr. Allen,
I am a student pastor. The Spirit of the Lord is working, because the Lord has laid the burden of prayer on the people. But the young converts really need more solid teaching. This is where I am sure you can help our whole assembly by sending literature for new converts, and for soul-winning, and for follow up. I thank the Lord for your work.

An urgent appeal from Uganda.

Dear Mr. Allen,
Thank you for your prayers. You have prayed for our nation. The Lord has answered our prayers, and we are free to worship the Lord. Brother, I beg of you to send me about sixteen thousand tracts, leaflets and booklets for spiritual help for our Christians. The people here in Uganda are hungry for the Word of God. I am an evangelist, and I have eighteen helpers in my ministry. Many people are coming to the Lord as Saviour, but we lack spiritual help. I beg for your help. The Lord will fulfil your needs. Hoping to hear from you soon. A slave for Jesus Christ.

These reports are only a selection of hundreds of requests and reports that arrived in the office every week. In the one month of July in 1979 they received several thousand letters. These brought news of more conversions and requests for still more leaflets and booklets. There seemed to be no limit to the amount of literature needed to meet the growing demand.

In light of these appeals, Mr. Allen led the team to focus on asking the Lord for another Multilith 1850 printer to help cope with the swell of appeals for more literature. The machine cost £6000. The expense of the machine in today's terms can be gauged when compared to the value of the large premises the Crusade had bought at £16,000. Added to this were the ongoing production costs which amounted to over £5,000 per month. Once more God did not fail them. The supporters expressed their confidence in the power of the gospel published on the printed page by generously endorsing the steady advance of the work.

It is a source of constant amazement that with nearly every big step forward that the Crusade took, the Lord supplied their need in an unusual way. Paying for the new machine and other equipment that was needed prompted one of these occasions. Ernie explained how God provided in a report in the "Good News" newsletter.

> For some time we have been asking you to pray for the work to grow in order that we would be able to send much more literature in answer to the hundreds of appeals that we receive. I am pleased to tell you that the work is growing. We have now sold the building at 285 Newtownards Road, and we received almost as much for it as we paid for the larger premises in Redcar Street. Because of this, we are now able to order more machines which will greatly speed up production.
>
> It has just come at the right time, for in this year 19,000 seeking souls wrote to us. This is by far the largest number of people we have ever heard from in any year of our ministry, and never before have we received so many thrilling testimonies of the Lord's blessing on the literature.

On another occasion when the Crusade was needing a considerable amount of money, even more than the cost of the printer, the Lord did something even more extraordinary. Although the Every Home Crusade is a non-profit organization and is a registered charity, it was subject to Value Added Tax (VAT) which cost them an extra 17.5% on all purchases. While the Crusade team was praying for a better printing press, Ernie and Samuel Adams looked at every possibility of being able to get the best deal possible. They considered the matter of this hefty tax levy which they had to pay. Samuel phoned the VAT office and made inquiries in relation to their status of non-profitability and as a registered charity. The civil servant was polite but explained that without the sales of literature above a certain amount the Crusade would not qualify for VAT rebate. However, the lady said she would forward the appropriate government literature about the eligibility and requirements. When the leaflet arrived, it affirmed that they did disqualify a normal charity from VAT exemption just as the lady had said. However, there was one clause that indicated that any charity that exported a large percentage of their product free of charge to third world countries would qualify for exemption. That fitted the role of the Every Home Crusade. Phone calls and letters shuttled to and from the government department until finally VAT exemption was granted to the Crusade. That truly was a giant step as they did not like to see the Lord's money spent on anything else other than literature.

While Samuel mulled over the process whereby he was able to acquire exemption, he remembered that VAT inspectors have a right to investigate a company's accounts and reclaim unpaid VAT for a period of up to seven years. Samuel reasoned that if this operated one way, then the same had to be valid in the other direction. He wrote again to the VAT department and pointed out that having gained VAT exempt status, they desired that the Crusade's payment of VAT for the previous seven years should be refunded.

Samuel's application for a refund set the office telephones buzzing. Many letters were exchanged between Every Home Crusade and the VAT department. It was a painstaking job to plough through the Crusade's accounts of the previous seven years and write out the details of the VAT account from recorded invoices. When this tedious task was completed the VAT inspectors came and combed through the Crusade's accounts for the previous seven years to verify the application which Samuel had submitted. They found that everything was in order. After the protracted investigation was completed, it was a happy day at the Every Home Crusade office when an envelope arrived from Her Majesty's Service containing a cheque for more than £48,000. This was a phenomenal amount, and they praised God for it.

On a regular basis God's work is sustained by the faithful, systematic and sacrificial giving of the Lord's people, many of whom do not seem to have a lot of material wealth. One such servant was a man called John. He lived in an ordinary terraced house in East Belfast. He was a hard worker all his life and never married. He lived modestly and frugally. One day a friend met John in a shop and found him bargaining for a better price for three oranges from the lady behind the counter. He was content to live a quiet life and look after himself. When he retired John had only one pastime - he loved to preach on the streets of the city and give out gospel leaflets to all and sundry.

One day he came to the Crusade factory at Redcar Street and showed interest in the print shop and all that went on in the building. Nothing gave Ernie more pleasure than to show friends round the premises and watch their reaction to the amount of work and volume of literature handled by the Crusade. John seemed to enjoy the visit to the factory and left without saying too much.

The next day he returned to the factory and went in to see Ernie in the small office where the correspondence was processed. He handed Ernie a gift of £1,000 for the work of the Crusade. Mr. Allen was surprised at the gift of such a large amount of money from this very plain and unassuming man. He was convinced the man had cleared his bank or Building Society accounts to give so sacrificially.

One week later, John returned and handed Ernie another envelope. It contained another gift of £1,000 for the Crusade. Ernie now felt this man was really going the extra mile. John explained that he wanted a good exchange rate for his money, he wanted to change pounds into "paper missionaries" to go all over the world.

When John returned to Redcar Street on the third week and again gave another £1,000 Ernie was astounded. John visited the Every Home Crusade every week for six weeks and left £1,000 on each visit. The sequence of weekly visits with gifts ceased for a few months, and then one day John returned with another £1,000 for the work of the gospel. On this visit John explained that he had worked hard all his life and had accumulated this money. At this advanced age in his life John said he did not need financial security and wanted to use his savings to spread the gospel. He told Ernie that his will had been signed, and he wanted whatever was left to be used to send leaflets around the world. Ernie thanked John, but pointed out that he needed to make sure he had enough to take care of his own needs.

When John became too ill to live alone Ernie arranged for him to be moved to a residential home. While John was resident in the home and until he died, Ernie attended to John's needs. After his home-call, the residue of John's estate was invested in the work of the Every Home Crusade. This was a very ordinary but wise man who, in an extraordinary way, made sure he laid up treasure in heaven.

His sentiments are summed up in a missionary hymn that can be sung to the tune of "Stand up, Stand up for Jesus."

Our Lord said, "Every creature."
How dare we disobey?
The message must be taken,
Then let us speed away.
The gospel must be published,
And put in every hand,
Oh, hasten then and seek them
Wherever they may roam.

We may not go in person,
But we can give and pray,
The printed page will tell them,
Of Christ the Truth, the Way.
Then let us put our money,
Where it will count the most,
The message is God's method,
His power the Holy Ghost.

Pastor and Mrs. Edward McClusky have been great supporters of the Crusade for many years. Until Mr. McClusky went to be with the Lord in 1998, they frequently visited the factory bringing gifts for the work and spending time in prayer with Ernie and Samuel. Since Mrs. McClusky was widowed she has continued to employ her skills as a seamstress to make handkerchief box covers from remnants of curtain material she picks up here and there. She produces these lovely decorative covers by the hundreds each year. They are sold to the public, and the full proceeds go to various missionary agencies. The Every Home Crusade is one of the benefactors of this Christian lady's enterprise to support the Lord's work by the work of her hands. Mrs. McClusky is a modern day Dorcas.

With these gifts the Crusade was able to purchase more equipment which increased the production of literature. Ernie wrote in the monthly newsletter: "I am pleased to tell you that we have taken delivery of a folding machine. Our printing department is now going better than ever. Hundreds of thousands of tracts are being printed. Humbly I appeal for your continued financial support as we seek to reach millions of souls with the gospel message through the printed page."

The Lord has provided for the needs of the Crusade in many ways. Sometimes it has been through large financial gifts from several donors. However, the main support of Every Home Crusade comes from hundreds of supporters, many of them pensioners, who sacrificially give smaller amounts to make sure the Word of God goes into all the world.

With several printers and a folding machine, the Crusade was equipped to produce all the leaflets needed, but they were still very dependent on the Outlook Press in Rathfriland for providing plates and making booklets. While the friends in Rathfriland were very helpful, the arrangement was not very convenient. This situation was made a focused point for prayer.

Initially the Crusade aimed to be able to produce their own plates. A reprographic camera was bought as well as the necessary apparatus for the developing process. After another short training seminar, Samuel became proficient at producing plates for the Crusade's print factory. This acquired skill not only helped speed up the printing process, but it became less expensive to provide the printing plates.

Samuel Adams took advantage of all the training courses offered each time a new machine was purchased and then passed those skills on to others at the literature factory. He also became adept at repairing and maintaining the machinery. The Multilith presses gave a lot of problems and broke down quite frequently. To bring an engineer to the factory not only cost a lot of money, but held up production when one was not available immediately.

Samuel did not consider himself to be very mechanical, but before long he was able to disassemble the various pieces of machinery, diagnose the problem, fix it and reassemble the unit so that it functioned perfectly again. Time and money that might have been spent on service and repairs was directed to the main thrust of the work - getting the gospel out by the printed page.

They purchased advanced computerised type-setting equipment which was modern for that day. This early computer was very limited in its scope and had several disadvantages, but again Samuel learned the techniques and was able to put it to good use.

Tonnes of paper were purchased every month, and this had to be unloaded by hand and placed in the store. From there it had to be physically carried to the presses. The Lord supplied the need for a fork-lift and trolley to facilitate the transport of paper.

Working in the noisy print factory was not always easy. There was the temptation to look on their toil as drudgery as they were hidden from the public eye. Nevertheless, the Scriptures always came at the right time to encourage and revitalise them - their labours were not in vain in the Lord.

The work was really growing and God had provided all their needs in ways far beyond their imaginations.

Chapter Ten

How Many Tongues To Go?

Paper does not have legs, except when that paper is currency or a tract in your pocket. The printed paper ministry of the Every Home Crusade is dependent on distributors to carry the literature to every part of the world. These distributors range from missionaries who have left these shores, to national pastors and Christian workers in numerous countries. Many of these work in close co-operation with the Crusade.

Maizie Smyth is a missionary in the Democratic Republic of Congo with UFM Worldwide. Maizie is a firebrand, full of zeal and enthusiasm for evangelism. She works in close association with Every Home Crusade and has used their literature extensively. She wrote from the Democratic Republic of Congo:

> I had just arrived in Kisangani as a new missionary, and it was soon evident that the one question that everyone was asking was, "Have you anything to give me to read?"

Government officials, policemen, soldiers, people at the market, they all were inquiring for reading material. We had just received several tonnes of gospel literature from Every Home Crusade, and it was thrilling to see the hunger for the Word of God.

Kisangani is located on the River Congo. We have congregations on both sides of this great river. One day I was crossing it on the government ferry. I was not alone - there were at least four hundred other people on board the large metal barge. I thought, "This would be a great place to give out tracts." I had an adequate supply with me, so I started to hand them out. I had only started distributing the leaflets when suddenly, it seemed that all four hundred people rushed to my side with their hands extended trying to grasp a tract. They did not want to miss out on something that was being given away.

All of a sudden there was panic. The sheer weight of so many people all rushing at one time to the side of the ferry caused the vessel to lurch to a very acute angle. From the ferry's bridge the captain sounded a blast on the piercing horn and continued to let it blow for what seemed ages. We immediately scattered all over the ferry again and brought the vessel upright. We were fairly shaken, but all was well.

I felt rather sheepish as I watched the captain make his way towards me. I knew I was the culprit but was not sure what the captain of the vessel was going to say. I was pleasantly surprised when he called me over to where he stood in the middle of the barge. "Start distributing your tracts from here," he snapped. "But I need to get some first."

There were five officers on duty. After I gave the Captain a leaflet he said, "Give me five more, one for each officer, please." Inwardly I prayed, "Thank you Lord for keeping us safe, thank you for giving me grace in that man's eyes, but thank you most of all for those who supply these tracts which give people the opportunity of reading the good news of the gospel."

One day Pastor Etape was sad as he watched yet another false cult make claims upon the uneducated believers in the Bumba region of Congo. If only someone could clearly present what God's Word says about what these false teachers are teaching. It was out of this frustration that the idea was born in his mind to write a defence against these false doctrines.

Etape set to work writing a tract in Swahili, "'The Teachings of False Cults in the Light of God's Word." This African pastor knew the value of the printed page. For many years he had used tracts which were supplied by the Every Home Crusade.

When he had finished, Pastor Etape made the five hundred mile journey to the church headquarters in Kisangani. He brought with him the manuscript of his new tract and asked me if I could get it printed somewhere, or somehow, as so many people needed to read a clear presentation of what these cults were really teaching.

I am their link between the Congolese Church and the Every Home Crusade, so I discussed with Mr. Allen and Samuel Adams if this tract could be printed. Soon it was rolling off the press and on its way to the Congo.

Some months later as we sat around the dying embers of the evening's fire in Bumba, Pastor Mehuma asked Pastor Etape, "Have you any more of those tracts - the ones that explain about the lies these cults are teaching? They have been such a blessing to us in our church in Banalia. The Branhamites have come to our town to start their assembly and are pulling our young people away at an alarming rate. Amongst their teachings, they say that Jesus could not have been human as He had no birth date. That little tract answers all of these questions.

"Recently a whole family just stopped coming to our church. I went to visit them, and they almost threw me out and told me that when they found the Branhamites they had found the true church. Before I left I gave them this same tract and continued to pray for them.

"Last Sunday at testimony time I saw the man and five of his children make their way to the front of the church to sing, Yesu Ye Moninga Na bato na Mabel. (Jesus You are the Friend of Bad People) As I sat in the pulpit, I listened intently as the father told how his whole family had been snatched away by these false teachings."

"However," he went on to say, 'one day during the cool period before dusk, I read a little tract that clearly presented what God's Word said in answer to what was being taught in this new assembly. Soon I got my Bible and read for myself that indeed I was mistaken. I gathered my little family around me, and we studied the tract and the Bible together. I called the elder Liaba, and we prayed together for God's forgiveness.'"

"Thank you Lord for those who produce such writings for us. The devil wants to pull us away from walking with Jesus but thank you for those markers that bring us back to the way. Thank you Every Home Crusade and especially for the vision that God gave to Mr. Ernie Allen to reach a world in need through the written page."

Such sincere reports stirred Ernie's heart to ask the Lord to help them reach still more people with the gospel of the Lord Jesus Christ.

With an increasing number of requests and pleas for literature coming from abroad, something had to be done to let them work more efficiently. Three developments speeded up the production and circulation of the literature even more.

The Multilith presses had served their purpose very well. However, the work and demands had moved on a lot. These presses, although not really old, frequently broke down and needed new parts.

Even though Samuel was able to repair the presses, they were not dependable enough to cope with the work that needed to be done. It was like asking a small car to do the work of a large truck. The Crusade needed to move on to a greater production rate, and for this more efficient presses were needed.

The Heidelberg presses were recognised in the printing trade as the Rolls Royce of machines. Ernie and Samuel felt that the Lord's work was worthy of the best and should be done as efficiently as possible. There was no other way forward other than to purchase a new Heidelberg G.T.O. 52.

For Every Home Crusade the cost of the new printing machine was astronomical, and this was by far the biggest challenge they had faced in their twenty years history, but they rested on God's provision in the past and put their faith in Him. The Redcar Street building when purchased cost £16,000 which God in His own way provided. Two years later the Heidelberg G.T.O. 52 cost £23,000. To procure this was a giant leap of faith, but the machine was necessary to enhance the printing programme. There were no other means to raise funds other than prayer and to inform the supporters. The Christian friends responded to the appeal, and the Lord, in many and varied ways, supplied the need.

You can imagine the excitement and awe among the Crusade team when the first Heidelberg was installed in the Redcar Street Factory. The Heidelberg machine arrived two weeks earlier than was originally planned. Ernie and Kathleen were on holiday in Scotland when the new press was to be installed, but as soon as Ernie heard that the press was arriving early he abandoned his holiday and came straight home. He has never gone on holiday since.

Clive Allen's return to the factory after spending a year on the fishing trawlers in Portavogie coincided with the arrival of the new press. His expertise was appreciated, and this was a major boost to the production team. Soon a new folding machine which cost £15,000 was added to the literature factory, and this speeded up the production even further. In the following year the output of literature far surpassed anything that had been accomplished previously. Over 12,000,000 publications comprising of gospel tracts, revival leaflets and Scripture booklets were published that year.

The next major development resulted in a wave of great blessing around the world. Although the Crusade team had greatly increased their capacity to produce printed material, this did not necessarily enable them to meet all the requests which were constantly coming to them. Many people wrote from Third World countries asking for copies of the Scriptures. The Crusade did not have the means to produce Bibles. Furthermore, if they did, it would be too a big drain on resources. Every Home Crusade's most popular booklet at that time was "Pardon and Assurance," which had been written by W. J. Patton from Dromara. Millions of copies of this booklet had been sent all over the world, and its message was the means for reaching and winning thousands of souls to Jesus Christ. However, Ernie recognised that the booklet was no substitute for the Scriptures.

One day while Ernie was in his office reading the mail, praying and thinking about those who repeatedly appealed for the Scriptures, his heart became heavy because he could not meet this need. It seemed just then he had a moment of inspiration. If I cannot give the people a whole Bible, why not give them a synopsis of the Bible message? If I cannot offer these hungry souls the whole loaf, at least I could offer them slices of bread. It was this thought that motivated Ernie to put together a booklet that was called "The Way of Salvation through our Lord Jesus Christ."

The Way of Salvation through our Lord Jesus Christ
Contents: All Scripture

God Created The Heaven And The Earth
I Was Afraid And I Hid Myself
God Spake All These Words
Thou Shalt Call His Name Jesus

Ye Must Be Born Again
And They Began To Be Merry
Many Mansions
The True Vine
One Of You Shall Betray Me
They Cried Out Saying, Crucify Him
He Is Not Here, He Is Risen
The Day Of Pentecost Was Fully Come
Lord, What Wilt Thou Have Me To Do?
Jesus Christ, Whom Having Not Seen Ye Love
A New Heaven And A New Earth

This is a sixteen page booklet, and on each of the fourteen inside pages there are Bible quotations in two columns. Inside the cover the first page is comprised of Genesis 1 and 2 giving the story of Creation. Page two gives the details of the fall of man into sin as told in Genesis chapter 3. The third page contains Exodus 19 and 20 giving an account of God giving Moses the Ten Commandments on Mount Sinai. Page four explains the virgin birth of the Lord Jesus Christ using the narrative of Luke 1 and 2. Page five is taken from John 3 with the Saviour's narrative about the new birth and the best known verse in the Bible, John 3:16. Page six recounts the parables of our Lord in Luke 15 and the account of the rich man and Lazarus in Luke 16. Page seven contains the teaching of our Lord about heaven and the Holy Spirit in John 14 and 15. Page eight gives an account of the agony of Gethsemane and the betrayal of the Lord Jesus from Mark 14. Page nine gives John's account of the crucifixion of our Lord from John 19. Page ten majors on the resurrection of the Lord Jesus and the Great Commission to the church as found in Matthew 28. Page eleven features the story of Pentecost as told in Acts 2 and the conversion of Saul of Tarsus in Acts 9. Pages twelve and thirteen are a selection of Scriptures from I Peter, I and II Corinthians and Romans relating to the Christian life. Page fourteen contains a description of heaven taken from the last two chapters of the Bible. The final page gives instructions of the way of salvation in "How to become a Christian."

This booklet was first put together in March 1981, and it was sent out under an adopted programme known as, "Mission to Millions." The title of the programme was most appropriate for the booklet has been published in scores of millions of copies, in seventy languages, and almost twenty years after it was published, this Scripture booklet is still reaping a great harvest of converts in many countries. Along with the next edition of "Good News," the monthly prayer leaflet of the Every Home Crusade, Ernie sent a copy of the booklet to the supporters of the Crusade with the following note; "With this letter I am pleased to send you a copy of the Scripture booklet, 'The Way of Salvation Through Our Lord Jesus Christ.' We continually receive many appeals for the supply of Bibles and New Testaments. We cannot afford to send Bibles to so many people, but this booklet has been specially prepared to contain the essential gospel message and to help lead souls to trust the Lord Jesus Christ as Saviour. The booklet has been prepared for circulation overseas in order to help meet the demand for the Scriptures."

This booklet was soon followed by a similar publication under the "Mission to Millions" programme. "The Gospel of Jesus Christ, the Light of the World" is based on the New Testament. Ernie wanted to produce a booklet that majored on the teachings of the Lord Jesus Christ and highlighted the principle points in His life, death and resurrection. The concluding pages of the booklet introduce selections from the New Testament Epistles and Revelation.

Requests also poured in from all over the world asking for copies of the Gospel of John for use in evangelism. Since they did not have this in print, the Crusade sent "The Way of Salvation" and "The Gospel of Jesus Christ" booklets instead. They were aware that there was a need for this tool of evangelism. One day Stanley Hodge, the Managing Director of Hodge Office Equipment, arrived at the Every Home Crusade office and presented a copy of the Gospel of John with two extra pages which provided seven simple lessons on the way of salvation. Ernie was impressed with the lay out of the booklet and the clarity of the instructions. Immediately it was adopted as another publication of the Every Home Crusade. Since then millions of "The Gospel of John - Seven Steps to Knowing God," have been printed and shipped all over the world in multiple languages.

These Gospel of John booklets began to run off the presses in millions and were dispatched around the globe. Soon letters began to arrive telling of the impact the gospel was making on many readers.

The next step that brought a significant increase in results was publishing the two new Scripture booklets in foreign languages. For almost twenty-five years the Every Home Crusade had published tens of millions of printed items, but they had all been in the English language. Ernie was aware that ninety per cent of all Christian literature published was for the English speaking world which made up a minority of the world's population. He prayed that the Lord would help them redress this imbalance.

About that time many letters began to arrive from Tanzania and Kenya asking for literature in Swahili. Until this juncture, no translators were available to supervise foreign language booklets. However, the simple nature of the new booklet, "The Way of Salvation," facilitated using pages out of a Swahili Bible and placing them in the appropriate sections. This was done in Belfast, and the original manuscript was sent to missionaries for correction. After the booklet completed a language check, thousands of them were published in Swahili and sent to missionaries in Tanzania and Kenya.

Requests then came from Africa to publish "The Way of Salvation" in the Bangala language. Eric Magowan and Maizie Smyth also requested 50,000 of the booklets in Zaire Swahili. From then on an avalanche of requests for these booklets in various languages started to come through. After the composition and correction of the booklets, the Crusade sent the translated literature to the respective countries involved.

The final development to speed up production happened with Maizie's and Eric's order for 50,000 copies of "The Way of

Salvation" for Zaire. The sixteen page booklet not only had to be folded, but it needed to be machine stapled. This presented a bottle neck in the production process because the only way they had to staple them was to slowly and painstakingly staple them one by one. To staple 50,000 booklets in this way was not only impractical, but it was a great impediment for other orders.

Samuel inquired if the process could be speeded up by incorporating the action of the wire stapler with the folding process. Engineers who had been working with these machines for years told him it could not be done. Samuel prayed about it and thought hard. He prayed some more and felt there must be a way to speed up the stapling process. Just then a second hand print-shop stitching machine became available, and Samuel bought it. He had a metal frame custom made to fit onto the folding machine. The stitching machine was then firmly placed upside down under the folder, and a series of belts and electric solenoids were linked between the folder and the stitching machine. Samuel persisted through a period of trial and error, until finally he succeeded in perfecting the process. The result was that the booklets could be stapled and folded in one operation of the same machine at a much accelerated pace. Samuel's hard work and persistence paid of, and he had accomplished his goal.

When seasoned engineers heard of this invention they came to see the machine working for themselves. Some of them took their caps off and scratched their heads for they had thought it could not be done. They looked on incredulously as stapler and folder operated in one action before their eyes. This presented to Ernie and Samuel an opportunity to witness to unbelieving printing tradesmen. Several of these professionals advised Samuel to patent his invention, but technology would soon overtake this ingenious contraption.

The production of "The Way of Salvation" booklet coincided with a great literacy drive in many countries. Millions of people were learning to read for the first time, and they were hungry for simple reading material. Through missionary contacts in these countries, Every Home Crusade was able to take full advantage of this situation and supply Scripture booklets to be put in the hands of these people. Ernie highlighted to friends that £5 would provide one hundred Scripture booklets or one thousand gospel tracts in a foreign language. Supporters of the work rose to the challenge and sent their gifts to encourage this work.

The Lord provided the means for another Heidelberg press to be installed at the Crusade's printing factory. The extra machinery ran almost non-stop every week. One Heidelberg printed up to 160,000 gospel tracts per day and gave a better quality production. However, this also meant that more personnel were needed to man the equipment.

By 1984 there were nine full-time workers on the staff at Redcar Street. Production had increased to three quarters of a tonne of literature every week. New gospel tracts with simple and clear instructions on the way of salvation were being introduced continually.

The Crusade placed orders for paper in quantities of seven tonnes which at that time cost £4,200. When the seven tonnes of paper arrived at Redcar Street most of the team had to take time out of their busy day to carry it into the store for they had no other means of unloading. Twenty-five tonnes of paper were used during the year, and this bulk of paper was soon transformed into Scripture and gospel publications which were sent to twenty countries abroad. It took £2,000 per week to maintain the ministry. Nearly £500 of this went to pay for postage and freight every five days. The operation was growing each day, and the results certainly justified the expense.

For over a decade Mr. & Mrs. Noel Turkington used Every Home Crusade literature in many parts of Ireland. They wrote to the Crusade to tell them of how the literature was being used and how it was blessing many.

> Dear Brother Allen,
>
> This year from January to May we visited many homes with gospel literature in the border areas of South Armagh

and South Tyrone. We also visited many homes near Armagh City and around Dungannon. In June we crossed the border into the South of Ireland for our summer work. We visited many homes of the Roman Catholic people in counties Cavan, Leitrim, Longford and Donegal. We then entered into Co. Mayo and went as far as Achill Island. It was a privilege to go forth with Bibles, New Testaments and booklets. It was a great blessing to have with us a good supply of Every Home Crusade gospel tracts. Very seldom did any person refuse a gospel tract. Please remember us in prayer as we continue in this ministry.

Every month more than 1,500 letters arrived for Ernie from people seeking to know the way of salvation.

Port Harcourt, Nigeria

I have seen the important role tracts have played in helping to bring me and others to the knowledge of the Saviour. Before I was converted I used to read and collect gospel tracts. As I read them, I was troubled about my sins until I gave my heart to Jesus. Please send me copies of "Pardon and Assurance" and other leaflets. Rejoice with me! God bless you all in Jesus' name and keep us going forward till the coming of our dear Lord Jesus.

Ghana, West Africa

I was a Moslem, but through reading your tracts the Lord has changed me into a Christian. I told my father that I wanted to be a Christian. He got so much annoyed that he had me tied to a tree, and I was beaten mercilessly. He then asked me if I still wanted to be a Christian. I said, "Yes, I will be a Christian until I die." He then ordered me to leave home. Since then I have been struggling to make a living. I strongly believe that one day I will come out of this time of trial. I remain yours truly.

Italy

I received your gospel tract, "God's Judgement Day," with the invitation to come to know the Lord Jesus Christ as my Saviour. I write to say that I have come to know Him, and I have been born again. It was and is very wonderful. Excuse me if I cannot write English very well. After reading your tract, I did as best I could accept the Lord Jesus as my Saviour, and I gave Him my life. Please send me the booklet, "Pardon for Sin and Assurance of Peace with God." I am sure it can help to make my faith bigger. (sic)

Six police officers saved

A most wonderful incident happened in connection with the reading of your booklet, "The Way of the Cross." I gave a copy to a police officer, and we talked together of the love of God and about the way of salvation. The police officer then trusted in the Lord Jesus as his Saviour. Then he took the booklet to the Police Station, and five of his friends also read the booklet, confessed their sins and trusted the Lord Jesus Christ as Saviour. The six of them were later baptised. This is the wonderful work of the Holy Spirit. Praise the Lord!

A witch doctor won to the Saviour

One Sunday I was reading to my family your tracts, "The Trumpet of God Will Sound," and "The Value of Your Soul." A witch doctor called at my home, and I gave him the tracts to read - he was an idol and juju worshipper. I prayed with him. He then prayed non-stop until the Holy Spirit fell upon him, and he confessed his sins. He trusted in the Lord Jesus as Saviour and burned all his idols and jujus. Praise the Lord!

A mother's thrilling testimony from Co. Londonderry

Just a wee note to thank you for the work you are doing for God. It was through reading your tracts and the witness of Mr. S. Linton that the Holy Spirit convicted me of sin. I praise God that He brought me to Himself and saved me one Sunday afternoon. Since then I have enjoyed the happiest time of my life. My children have seen the great change in the home and in my life. Sometimes I can hardly believe that it is all true. I could write a book about what the Lord has been doing. My two sisters have been saved; my three children have been saved; my mother and her two sisters have professed to be saved. God bless you Mr. Allen in your service for our Lord Jesus Christ.

A young convert in Uganda won forty-two people to the Saviour

I praise the Lord for you there in the work of bringing people to the Saviour. Thank you very much for the literature which I received in the month of June. I read them carefully. When I read the booklet "Pardon and Assurance" and the leaflets I repented from all my sins, and I accepted the Lord Jesus to be my personal Saviour. I opened my heart to receive God's counsel and guidance for my new life in Jesus. From that day, 13th July, I began to speak to others about the Lord Jesus Christ. I told them what great things the Lord had done for me. Sir, this is another result of your leaflets - from 13th July to 23rd of August, forty-two persons have repented and have professed to be saved. Please send me leaflets and booklets for these forty-two converts.

Yours faithfully in the Matchless Name of our Lord Jesus Christ.

There were hundreds more such letters reporting what the Lord was doing through the printed pages which had been sent from the Every Home Crusade at Redcar Street. God's promise of blessing on Ernie's life and ministry was being realised far beyond what might have happened had he remained in the pastoral ministry.

Chapter Eleven

FAITH FACES OBSTACLES

Samuel Rutherford, the Scottish divine whose writings have inspired many suffering saints and who faced many painful trials, wrote, "Praise God for the hammer, the file and the furnace." There are few men of God who escape being submitted to painful trials where it seems that hammer blows pound the soul, the file shapes the character and the furnace melts the heart. These are tools God uses to conform His children to more likeness to Christ. Job felt it when he declared, "When He has tried me I will come forth as gold."

The Scriptures remind us that God has put "His treasure in earthen vessels that the excellency of the power may be of God and not of us." Paul continued, "We are troubled on every side...always bearing about in the body the dying of the Lord Jesus...we are always delivered on to death." (2 Corinthians 4:7-11) Satan cannot touch the heavenly treasure which the Christian has within him, but there are times when God permits Satan to buffet the vessel, our physical body. God often uses the buffeting for our blessing. When you are a soldier of Jesus Christ and a follower of the Lamb, you should not be surprised when you have to face the hammer, the file and the furnace. God has His purpose.

The monthly "Good News" report of the Crusade continued to inform supporters of the tonnes of literature that were being shipped to various countries around the globe and to give excerpts from the hundreds of letters that arrived from distant shores. In the September 1985 edition there was a happy event to record, and at the same time some sad news to disclose. The good news was of the marriage of Samuel Adams to Carol French. It carried a photograph of the couple of their wedding day, 12th September 1985, and this was an occasion for great happiness. Carol worked at the Child Evangelism Fellowship as a local CEF director in the Laganvalley area, but later she joined the Every Home Crusade office staff where she still fulfils various duties.

Samuel had been with the Every Home Crusade for seven years and had developed skills which greatly assisted Mr. Allen. That assistance was very much needed at that time for tucked in at the end of the same edition of "Good News" was a snippet of personal news from Ernie.

> Recently I found that I needed to have radio-therapy treatment for my throat. This course of treatment has been almost completed, and I am very grateful to all the friends who have been praying for me at this time. Please continue to pray for a full and complete recovery for His Service and for His Glory. It has been a wonderful privilege to serve our Lord Jesus Christ in the past years in the worldwide ministry of the printed page, and I believe that He has much more work for me to do for Him in the coming days. In the meantime, the work goes on steadily day-by-day, and I am very grateful to have the help of our fine team of full-time and part-time helpers.

This was the first mention of a problem that had been dogging Ernie for several months. It was typical of the man that he should play down news of a serious illness. In the spring of that year he had developed a hoarseness in his voice without any other usual symptoms of a cold or influenza. He insisted on continuing with his involvement at the factory and tried to mask his true condition from his family and friends. As weeks went by, the rasping feeling in his throat got so bad that while he was speaking at a meeting in Carryduff, he had to stop in the middle of his preaching. As a result, Ernie had to refrain from public speaking engagements. His family insisted that he see a consultant.

An appointment was made, and over a course of several weeks, Ernie underwent extensive examinations and tests. He finally had an operation under general anaesthetic at the Ulster Clinic, Belfast. A tumour was removed from Ernie's larynx, and a biopsy was sent to the laboratory for further investigation. When the result returned, Mr. Stewart, the surgeon, disclosed to Ernie that the tumour he had removed from his larynx was malignant.

Ernie was alone when the surgeon broke this news to him. Instead of his heart slumping in despair, his soul was momentarily lifted up to God in prayer to ask for Divine intervention. His thoughts went to Kathleen and his children, and how would they face this news. He knew that other good friends had wrestled with coming to terms with what was commonly known as the "big C."

He thought of the work of the Crusade and how it was rapidly developing. Ernie, forever the optimist and in spite of the foreboding in the dark predictions and prognosis, refused to believe that his work at the Crusade was finished. God had called him, and he felt there was still a lot of work to do. He said to himself, "A man is immortal until his work is finished. Lord I have work still to do."

Kathleen and the family were stunned at the news. They admired Ernie's faith and stood with him in prayer, but they were not unaware that many had lost their voice because of this malady, and others had died as a result of this same condition.

At the factory the news was received with shock. A minister disclosed to Samuel that Ernie was an extremely ill man, and only the touch of God could raise him up again. This news caused the team to immediately seek the Lord in prayer for the beloved leader of the work. Every Home Crusade had been Ernie's life. Every waking moment was spent with this work uppermost in his mind.

Ernie preferred not to say too much to the general public, but he wrote of the experience.

> After serving our Lord Jesus Christ in the ministry of the printed page for many years, in the Spring of 1985 I began to have serious trouble with my voice. In the month of August of that year I went through an operation in which a growth was removed from my throat. This growth proved to be malignant, and in the following month I received a course of radiotherapy treatment in Belvoir Park Hospital.
>
> It was a very solemn experience to realise that cancer had begun in my throat. Day by day I was walking with death. The consultant told me that I had little chance of recovery. He also said that they expected to have to remove my voice box. The surgeon explained what this operation would involve and what the likely outcome would mean - I would not be able to speak again and would need a small microphone to place at my throat. While in the Belvoir Park Hospital I saw men who had been through this operation. I felt that death had grabbed me by the throat, and I would rather die than lose my voice.
>
> Even in those dark days I knew that God had called me to His service, and that my work was not finished. From the end of September, I began to seek the Lord in prayer and fasting. I prayed that He would heal my throat and give me the health and strength to complete the work He had committed to me. I wanted to see the vision fulfilled which He had graciously given to me as a young man.

During the following weeks and months, I knew that hundreds of our friends in the Every Home Crusade fellowship were also praying that the Lord would restore me to health and strength. I remember at that time, looking at my car, and wondering if I would ever be able to drive it again. Day by day as I prayed and fasted; the petition of my heart was,

"Lord, let me live to preach Thy Word,
And let me to Thy glory live,
My every sacred moment spend,
In publishing the sinner's Friend."

In the November and December issues of "Good News" priority was given to news of converts and appeals for literature from around the world. From his home and the hospital, Ernie just gave brief updates of his condition at the end of each report.

November, 1985: "On 21st of the month I had my first check-up at the Hospital, and I was given a very good and encouraging report of the condition of my throat. Please continue to pray for a full recovery of health and strength and voice."

December 1985: "I would like to thank all the friends who have been praying for my healing and recovery. I am feeling very well and am now able to take more part in the work. Please pray on for a full recovery of health and voice for His glory and for His service."

These reports actually covered up how low Ernie really was feeling. His strength was drained from him, and he could not conduct any sort of conversation. However, the Every Home Crusade was the priority in his life, and he felt that work must continue unhindered.

The Allen family made the Christmas season a special time at home, but Ernie was not a well man. The end of the year filled their hearts with gratitude that the Lord had brought them through these difficulties. Looking into the New Year, the question of a secondary manifestation of the malignancy remained unanswered. This kept the family, the team and many friends praying for Ernie's full recovery.

The concern of those days was punctuated by his frequent visits to the hospital.

> At regular intervals I went to the Royal Victoria Hospital for check-ups. In December the surgeon told me that he wanted me to go into the Ulster Hospital at Dundonald to examine my throat under anesthetic in the operating theatre. In those days I lived in the Bible. I read of answers to prayer in the lives of God's servants in the Old Testament. I also read of the healing ministry of our Lord Jesus Christ. I was dwelling and resting on the promises of God.

When he went to the Ulster Hospital early in January he was at a very low ebb, and although earnest prayers were made for him his family and friends were not optimistic. They did not know what the outcome would be. Ernie wrote:

> On 7th January I arrived at the hospital, and I very well remember waiting to be taken into the operating theatre. I knew that beyond those doors the answer would be either life or death. My hope was in the Lord that He would answer prayer and enable me to complete my ministry in His service.
>
> In the afternoon after the examination the surgeon came to my bedside, and he said to me, "Mr. Allen, all is clear."
>
> I asked him, "Mr. Stewart, you know that I do a bit of preaching. When could I commence preaching again ?"
>
> He replied, "I think you could begin next week."
>
> "Therefore, saith the Lord, Turn ye to Me with all your heart, and with fasting, and with weeping. Rend your heart, and turn unto the Lord your God: for He is gracious and merciful, slow to anger, and of great kindness." (Joel 2 - 12,13) My heart was now full of gratitude and worship to the Lord, for I had proved the truth of these words.

The Lord had turned around what seemed to be an impossible situation. Ernie experienced what the hospital called "an accelerated recovery." Within months he was back at his desk giving leadership to the Crusade. He and the family recognised that this was the hand of God in answer to many prayers that had been offered by friends and supporters and gave God the glory. The Lord had brought Ernie and his family through the dark days, but this was a sure indication that the same Lord Jesus still had future plans for the work of Every Home Crusade.

This was certainly a triumph of faith; however, not all cases of those who experience cancer end in success. The peaks and valleys of our Christian experience teach us that sometimes the triumphs of faith appear on the natural level as human tragedy.

The author of Hebrews wrote, "By faith Abraham, when he was tried, offered up Isaac: and he that had received the promises offered up his only begotten son,...accounting that God was able to raise him up, even from the dead; from whence also he received him in a figure." (Hebrews 11:17-19) Not everyone whose faith has been tried has received the same deliverance. The author of Hebrews also spoke of others who "were tortured, not accepting deliverance; that they might obtain a better resurrection." (Hebrews 11:35)

Ernie Allen had passed through a deep valley of trial and sickness but had come through to shine again in the service of His Lord. Another trial was soon to touch the Every Home Crusade that climaxed in a different conclusion. It also was triumph, but it came through tragedy.

Fred Starrett joined the Every Home Crusade in 1982. With the expansion of the work after their arrival in Redcar Street, Ernie was always on the lookout for suitable staff. David McIlveen, minister of Sandown Road Free Presbyterian Church, suggested that Freddie would be a suitable young man as he was just about to leave school. Freddie was reared in East Belfast and was converted as a boy at Sunday School. As a Christian teenager he was friendly, outgoing and was not ashamed to identify himself as a follower of the Lord Jesus Christ.

Freddie embraced the opportunity to engage in the Lord's service when he was approached about working in the Every Home Crusade print factory. Like all new employees Freddie began his career at the factory by wrapping and addressing parcels in the dispatch department. It soon became evident to all that this young man aimed for excellence and quality in all that he set his hand to do. He was not only competent at his job but was extremely tidy in his dress and neat in his workmanship. He quickly moved on to learn how to operate the new folding machine, and from there he learned printing skills on the factory floor.

Frequently Ernie invited some of the factory team to accompany him on deputation meetings. He involved them by asking them to either pray, give their testimony or give a report of their work with the Every Home Crusade.

Not long after Freddie arrived at the Redcar Street print factory Ernie took Freddie along to one of the deputation meetings. He informed the young man in advance that he would be invited to open in prayer. After the opening hymn, Ernie called on Freddie to lead in prayer. The young man rose to his feet and prayed with passion and eloquence. Ernie had been in the Lord's work a long time and had seldom heard a young man pray in such a fluent and spontaneous way. After the meeting, Ernie complimented young Freddie and said, "I was really impressed with that prayer tonight."

Without a blush on his face, Freddie smiled and commented, "Did you like it? It is one of Spurgeon's prayers that I memorised."

Freddie's good memory was a great asset to him as he developed evident preaching skills. He began to conduct deputation meetings, show slides and preach wherever he was invited to do so. By the time he was in his early twenties life seemed to be shaping up well for this young man. He was involved in the Lord's work; he was active in his local church; he was developing his preaching skills and was going steady with a fine Christian girl.

After six years of working in Redcar Street, Freddie shared with Ernie and Samuel that he was thinking and praying about enlisting as a part-time soldier in the Ulster Defence Regiment, the Ulster regiment which was at that time on the front line against the ongoing terrorism in Northern Ireland. Ernie and Samuel discussed with him the pros and cons of such a move and pointed out the obvious dangers involved. Freddie explained that he had prayed about this matter and felt constrained to join as he was convinced this was God's will for him.

This young man wanted to make a legitimate contribution to restoring peace to Ulster and was persuaded this was his way of making a contribution to a resolution of the conflict. Furthermore, he felt that as a part-time soldier his duties would not distract from his commitment to the Every Home Crusade, and it would give him opportunity to mingle with soldiers to whom he would be able to speak of his faith in Jesus Christ.

In due course the young man was accepted into the regiment, and after his initial training he soon was armed and patrolling the troubled streets of Belfast with other soldiers. The Every Home Crusade team was a very closely knit body of young men under Ernie's leadership. All of them cared for each other and prayed for each other's needs and concerns. Freddie was a high priority in their prayers in face of the dangers to which he was exposed.

Freddie developed a special bond of friendship with his work colleague Paul Roberts. They enjoyed each other's humour and frequently encouraged each other when any problem or disappointment was encountered. Freddie was invited to be best man at Paul's wedding. Paul recalls his memories of his close friend. "He was a great person. He was neat and tidy in every way, but he was great fun to be with. Working in a print shop every day even though it is a Christian establishment makes it is easy to grow cold in your Christian life. It happened to me, but Freddie was always able to discern my coldness and then encouraged me to go on in my Christian life."

At 5:30 p.m. on Wednesday, 24th February 1988, Freddie finished his work at the print shop. He waved goodbye to Ernie and his work mates and rushed home. After a quick meal and wash, he headed to the barrack. He proudly donned his army uniform and reported for duty. Freddie was surprised to find that his regular duty had been changed to substitute for a soldier who was not able to be on duty that evening. In the place of the absent soldier Freddie accompanied three other UDR men into the city centre.

At that time the security gates at Belfast's city centre were closed at night to prevent terrorists planting car bombs in the heart of the city. At about half past eleven o'clock that cold and crisp winter night, while the army patrol vehicle waited nearby, Freddie and another soldier colleague went to shut and fasten the gates at the north end of Royal Avenue. Just as they approached the gate, a five hundred pound bomb which had been concealed behind advertising hoardings, was detonated. The horrific blast lifted the army vehicle into the air and ripped through the surrounding buildings scattering debris for hundreds of yards. The two young soldiers lay mortally wounded on the avenue.

Samuel Adams heard the blast just as he was getting ready for bed at his home eight miles away in Drumbo. He remembered Freddie was on duty and wondered if he had seen anything. Paul Roberts also heard the explosion and prayed for those who might be caught up in it. He also specifically prayed for Freddie as he had done on all other nights before he retired to bed. Ernie and Kathleen Allen who lived less than two miles from the scene of the explosion not only heard the blast, but the windows of their home shook.

In the pandemonium and confusion that immediately followed the explosion, soldiers and police hurried to aid their wounded colleagues. Freddie's colleague died instantly. An ambulance was on the scene in a few minutes, and Freddie was rushed to hospital. His family was called to the hospital only to see Freddie slip from this life into the presence of His Lord at around three o'clock on Thursday morning.

Samuel and Carol Adams were eating breakfast at seven thirty the next morning before Samuel made his customary journey to work. He turned on the radio to learn where the loud explosion had been the previous night. The news of yet another atrocity that resulted in carnage and death was sickening. When the broadcaster gave the names of the young soldiers who had died as a result of the tragedy both Samuel and Carol were dumb founded. Fred Starrett?

The radio presenter said that both young soldiers killed were full-time members of the UDR, and Samuel knew that Freddie was not full-time. In a grasp for some forlorn hope he suggested to Carol, "Maybe it is another Fred Starrett. I'll have to find out."

Samuel phoned Ernie to find out if he had heard anything. He said he just had received a call from his son-in-law, Norman Mercer, informing him of the news bulletin. Ernie was stunned, but he found it hard to believe that it was the Freddie Starrett that worked at the Every Home Crusade office. Samuel finally resorted to phoning Freddie's girlfriend's home hoping to gain news from her father. Samuel was shocked when it was Freddie's girlfriend who answered the phone, and she heart-breakingly confirmed the sad news that he had dreaded hearing.

All sorts of thoughts and emotions rushed through Samuel's mind. Freddie's winsome way, warm smile and hard work were going to leave a huge gap in the Crusade team. The young colleague's parents and sister would be devastated, and his girlfriend's heart would be broken.

Freddie's friend, Paul Roberts, was awakened early that Thursday morning by a phone call from his mother-in-law to let him know the fateful news. Paul could not take in that the news was true. How could it happen? Immediately he busied himself to go to the Crusade's premises in Redcar Street.

As the workers came in that morning, grief was written on their faces and tears flowed freely. Some only heard the sad news upon arrival at the factory. It seemed as though a heavy cloud of silence hung over the place. Ernie and Samuel led in prayer, but for some it was too painful to pray audibly. In almost hushed tones they talked of former times with their departed colleague. Freddie's friend Paul Roberts said the factory seemed like a ghost town that morning.

Ernie, Samuel and Freddie's other colleagues from the Crusade went to the Starrett home in Grand Parade to sympathise with Mr. & Mrs. Starrett and his sister Violet. Even though they knew that

Freddie had gone to be with his Lord, that Thursday was a sad day for every one. A life that was so useful, so promising and so lovely had been wiped out by evil men.

The funeral service at Sandown Road Free Presbyterian Church where Freddie had attended drew hundreds of people more than the building could accommodate. David McIlveen invited Ernie to take part in the service, but he was too crushed to do so. In his place, Samuel shared in the service which was conducted by Freddie's minister, David McIlveen and Dr. Ian Paisley. A few days after Freddie's death his father put his faith in Jesus Christ.

A week after the funeral the following insertion appeared under a photo of Freddie working at the printing press in the "Good News" monthly report:

> **The late Frederick Starrett at his work in the Every Home Crusade**
>
> I am very sorry to inform you of the sudden home call of our brother on Wednesday night, 24th of February as the result of an IRA explosion in Belfast. For over six years Freddie served our Lord Jesus Christ most faithfully in the work here. Let us pray for the members of his family and for all his friends and loved ones in this time of sad bereavement.

As the news of Freddie Starrett's death spread throughout the supporters of the Every Home Crusade, expressions of sympathy poured in. Many sent in gifts for the work in memory of the young man. Freddie had seen the work of the Crusade grow, and its influence for God become greater as the gospel went out in printed form. Ernie encouraged his grieving band of workers that the best tribute they could express to their fallen colleague was to keep at the work he enjoyed. Freddie Starrett had gone to be with his Lord, but the work of faith and enterprise of which he was a vital part and the machines he helped operate kept rolling out the message of the gospel of grace to a needy world.

Chapter Twelve

MEET THE TEAM

John Donne's familiar saying is appropriate when talking of the team at the Every Home Crusade headquarters. "No man is an island entire of itself; every man is a piece of the continent, a part of the main; if a clod be washed away by the sea, Europe is the less...any man's death diminishes me, because I am involved in mankind; and therefore, never send to know for whom the bell tolls, it tolls for thee."

Freddie Starrett's death diminished the number of staff at the Every Home Crusade, but his memory spurred them on to greater dedication to their work. The home going of God's servant also challenged others and resulted in them joining the Crusade team.

Robin McCulla had finished his training at the Faith Mission Bible School in Edinburgh. Since his conversion to Jesus Christ he felt God was calling him to be a missionary. He went into college with an interest in India, the second most populous country in the world. In the course of his studies the burden for India did not lessen, but the door to the sub-continent did not open for him. After a period conducting missions with the Faith Mission, he returned to college to work as the supervisor of the men students. This responsibility did not seem to fit into the plan he felt the Lord had for him, but he was prepared to wait for God's timing.

Robin's girlfriend, Elizabeth Martin, was from Northern Ireland and was a good friend of Carol Adams, Samuel's wife. When Robin returned home from college for a visit the young couple would often visited the Adams' home in Drumbo. Samuel was so impressed with them that he frequently remarked to Carol that Robin and Elizabeth would make fine workers with the Crusade. Without saying anything to them, the suggestion of joining the Crusade was turned into a matter of prayer at the Adams' home. Samuel waited for a convenient time to mention it to them.

Meanwhile back in Edinburgh Robin waited for God to open a door of ministry for him. Something was sure to happen, and it did. In the November edition of "Good News" in 1987 Robin read a report of how the Crusade had just taken delivery of a new press, and he realised there was a need for workers. He considered talking the matter over with Samuel while home at Christmas, however, when he arrived at their home for a visit he did not feel he should mention the matter.

While he waited on the Lord, he read Acts 16, and it seemed as though the Lord was saying to him, "Come over and help us." Robin was also responsible to give evangelistic leadership for the students at college, and he often used the Every Home Crusade tracts. During a half-term visit to Belfast in February 1988, Robin called at the Crusade offices at Redcar Street to pick up a supply of publications. He decided while he was there he would make an appointment to see Mr. Allen.

When Robin walked into the Redcar Street offices Samuel was surprised to see him. He felt he should approach Robin about what was on his heart. When Samuel suggested the possibility of joining the team, Robin was taken aback for that was the reason he was at the office. After an interview with Ernie and Samuel both parties felt sure that this Faith Mission worker was sent by the Lord, but there was no immediate vacancy. They proposed to Robin that he remain with the Faith Mission until a vacancy arose with the Crusade.

The young man left satisfied that the Lord was opening the door, but a bit restless about having to wait. He travelled back to Edinburgh that night. Ten days later he heard from a student of the tragic death of Freddie Starrett. Robin was not only stunned, he was shaken. When Samuel Adams phoned him there was a most subdued conversation about the tragedy and the mystery of God's will. At the end of the conversation Samuel spoke the words that were almost identical to that which God had given to Robin from Acts 16. "Come over and help us."

Robin was released of his duties with the Faith Mission in March 1988 and joined the Crusade team at Redcar Street. Like others before him he worked his way through the system, until he was introduced to the printing presses. He finally graduated to work on one of the most advanced machines. Looking back on God's leading Robin commented:

> Elizabeth and I did not go to India as missionaries, nor did we learn an oriental language, but I am part of a team which sends eighteen tonnes of literature in eleven different languages to India every month. I realise that through the many millions of pieces of literature the Every Home Crusade sends to India we have reached more people in India than I might have done had I spent my entire life there. The letters that we receive confirm the fact that the gospel by printed page is dynamic in its effect and leads many persons to know Jesus Christ as Saviour.

Robin works as a vital member of a larger team. All the workers admit that they need each other, and their fellowship encourages each other. Someone once said, "The reason mountain climbers are tied together is to keep the sane ones from going home." The workers kept each other revitalised.

The Church of Jesus Christ is likened to a body or a building whose parts are joined together and dependant on each other. That same principle is experienced at the Every Home Crusade. Every part of the work and all the workers are linked to each other. The leaders need the printers, who need the machinists, who need the dispatchers, who need the clerical workers, who need the distributors, who need the supporters, and they all need the Lord. Every Home Crusade is a family business - the Lord's family.

Paul Roberts joined the Every Home Crusade at the same time as his friend Freddie Starrett in 1982. The two East Belfast lads became firm friends. Paul is a tall and well built young man sporting a short beard, and he works at a Heidelberg 102ZP Perfecter press alongside Robin on the factory floor. He became part of the Lord's family when he was converted in 1980. Since early in his Christian life Paul wanted to serve the Lord.

Besides the impact his late colleague made on him, Paul feels that Ernie Allen has been one of the biggest inspirations in his life. He is amazed at Ernie's great faith in God, his great passion for the lost and his humility which attracts admiration from all the team members. Paul said, "Mr. Allen is like a father to us all. He is ever encouraging us at our work and always has time to listen to what we might have to say. It would be very hard to find a man of God equal to him. Samuel also is a great motivator to us all."

Although Paul has been working as a printer for more than seventeen years now, he has not lost the excitement and motivation of knowing that what is produced in the Every Home Crusade factory is yielding a great harvest for the Lord Jesus Christ all over the world. Paul expressed, "It is important that we function as a team and keep our eye on the goal. We aim to please the Lord and to reach the world."

Douglas Condell also operates a Heidelberg press at the factory. He was saved as a young teenager at Loughoonan Mission Hall in County Monaghan. Ernie Allen's name was familiar to him since his childhood for he was raised in a Christian home, and his parents hosted the Irish Evangelistic Band Prayer meeting in their home. Feeling God's call on his life, Douglas enrolled at the Faith Mission Bible College in 1980 and completed his studies there.

His first involvement with Every Home Crusade was in 1984 when he teamed up with his friend Adrian French under the auspices of the Every Home Crusade to place gospel literature in every home in County Cork. After his involvement in the distribution ministry, Douglas was transferred to work in the Redcar Street factory. He also progressed from packaging orders to printing. He presently has the responsibility for one of the three Heidelberg Perfecter machines which run every day.

Richard Garnham became part of the team of the Every Home Crusade at the end of a difficult year for him in1985. He had always treasured his Christian home and parents. Converted to Jesus Christ as a boy at school through the testimony of a fellow pupil, Richard was influenced by his mum and dad to put the Lord first in his life. His father often indicated to him the simple truth displayed on a plaque in their home, "Only one life, t'will soon be past. Only what's done for Jesus will last."

Tragically in 1984, Reggie Garnham, Richard's dad, a fireman, was killed when a tree fell on his car as he returned from an emergency call on a stormy night. His father's sudden death impressed upon Richard the importance of living every moment for the Lord Jesus Christ.

Later that same year, Richard was made redundant from the workshop where he was employed in Ballynahinch. It seemed that even though he believed that God worked all things together for good, nothing was working out for him. It was just then that the Lord opened a door to him that would introduce Richard into Christian service. Samuel Adams was aware that a young man in Ballynahinch had come through a difficult time and was available for work. He contacted Richard, and within a short time Richard joined the team in the factory at 52 Redcar Street.

He progressed through the various departments of the Crusade and learned the printing trade. Richard, like the other workers, periodically joined Ernie as part of the deputation team which visited various churches representing the Crusade. Before long it became evident that Richard had good communication skills and a good understanding of the Word of God. This led to opportunities for him to preach all over Northern Ireland.

Richard worked at the Crusade for fourteen years, and he felt the experience of working alongside Ernie Allen and the friends at the Every Home Crusade was a virtual training school in the life of faith. He learned from Ernie's emphasis on the centrality of the Word of God and his vision for the lost. He found that Ernie Allen was not aloof from people. He was warm and humble in his approach to people. These qualities prompted Richard to hold the leader of the Crusade in very high esteem as a mentor who helped shape his life and make him ready for his present pastoral responsibilities in Carr Baptist just outside Carryduff.

When Richard left the Crusade to assume his work as a pastor, Stephen Roberts, Paul Robert's brother, who was already a qualified printer was able to slot into the vacancy. His experience in the printing trade was very much appreciated.

In the dispatch room Ian De Courcy and David Megarry are surrounded with piles of folded booklets and tracts on one side and small cardboard boxes and large envelopes on the other. Music plays in the background as they busily fill envelopes and boxes with orders and then seal them. Appropriate address labels are placed on the parcels, and they are stacked in mail bags ready to be collected later by the Royal Mail van. Millions of pieces of literature are dispatched from this small room to the great world outside.

As in other parts of the factory where several colleagues work together, there is plenty of interaction between David and Ian. They discuss and share everything from weighty theological subjects to the latest news in the evangelical community, and at times they set the political world aright.

David was a farmer before he went to train at the Faith Mission Bible School in Edinburgh. He was aware of the work of the Crusade from his association with Bottear Mission Hall and the Moira

Missionary Convention. When Mr. Allen approached him to consider involvement with the Crusade team, David did not hesitate. Although he was used to the outdoor life on a farm, he counts it a privilege to work for the Lord in the dispatch room. When he closes a parcel of gospel literature which is bound for a foreign country, he imagines what it will be like for some one to open that same parcel in a distant land and discover the truth of the gospel of Jesus Christ, perhaps for the first time.

At the Crusade's literature factory David has several other responsibilities besides his work in the dispatch room. He is the principal fork-lift operator, and this keeps him very busy loading containers for shipments of literature to distant places or unloading new paper for the factory. David always has a song or a whistle as he shuttles back and forth between the Crusade's store and the factory floor, delivering printed material to deposit in the store or collecting paper needed for the print shop.

Ian, who is one of the latest recruits at the Crusade, was converted as a twelve year old boy and admits he owes much to his Christian parents. He claims that the monotony of packaging literature all day is balanced by the return mail that is constantly arriving at the Crusade's office reporting hundreds of conversions. Besides using tape and glue, every envelope and package is sealed with prayer.

In one of the smallest offices at the front of the building Timothy Millen, from the Maze area near Lisburn, is absorbed in his clerical responsibilities. Everyone acknowledges how suitable and proficient this young man is in his job. It was at an evangelistic coffee bar outreach at Priesthill Youth Club that Timothy was converted when he was twelve years old. After completing his degree at university, he joined the staff at the Crusade to serve the Lord. He spent a short period in dispatch, but his main work at the Crusade was operating the folding unit and the collating machine.

When Lorna Harpur left the Crusade, a vacancy was created in the secretarial area of the work. Someone with computer skills was needed urgently to replace Lorna. Timothy left the factory floor and accepted this responsibility. He fitted into this office very quickly and has fulfilled an efficient role processing files, recording gifts and attending to regular correspondence.

Timothy says he is very happy at his work because it is the Lord's work. "This is not what I would have chosen as a secular career, but my joy is to do the Lord's will." He continued, "For me it is a privilege to correspond with those who support the work and have first hand acquaintance by mail with many who have been saved through the ministry of the gospel by means of the printed page."

James "Junior" Hilland, operates the Heidelberg GTO52 and enjoys his job. Although he did not come from a Christian home Junior was greatly influenced through the witness of young people at his church in Ballynahinch. They encouraged him to attend a special meeting which Pastor Bill Dunn was conducting in Tullynore Mission Hall, near Hillsborough. Junior trusted the Lord Jesus as his Saviour at this meeting.

After training at the Faith Mission Bible College, Junior spent over two years in the Faith Mission evangelistic work conducting meetings in the Highlands and Border District of Scotland. In 1996 he returned to Northern Ireland with his wife Hazel, and they were unsure of what the Lord had in store for them in the future. After a short spell of working at the Castlewellan Conference Centre, Richard Garnham mentioned to Junior about openings in the Every Home Crusade. Junior found there was a place for him, and after gaining initial experience on the folding machine and the collator, Junior learned to run a printing press.

Paul McGuiggan from Lisburn was brought up in a good home and was always sent to church and Sunday School, but it was at a Scripture Union Camp in Kilkenny that he trusted the Saviour. After leaving school, Paul went to work as a plumber, but in his heart he felt the Lord wanted him in Christian work. He had often been challenged when members of the Every Home Crusade spoke at the Lisburn Congregational Church where he attended. He shared these thoughts with his pastor Norman Fox.

PHOTOGRAPHS

An Overall View of the Print Room

One of the many 18 Tonne Containers being loaded.

Scripture Booklets being distributed after an open air meeting in Nairobi.

Two Very large Services being conducted by "Jesus is Lord Fellowship" in the Philippines.

Some of the one and a half Million young people reached with the Gospel Message every year by India Bible Literature Mission.

One of the containers which we send every 4 weeks to India being unloaded.

A large evangelistic Crusade reaching some of the 1 Billion people in India.

Robin McCulla operating one of our Folding Machines.

Children of Romania who received some of the two million Gospel leaflets as seen below with Mr & Mrs Tom Sommerville in our factory.

The Muller Saddle Stitcher which produces 50,000 Gospels of John in one day.

The Gospel being presented to the people of Peru.

Empty Hands reaching for the Gospel Message in Russia.

One of the Great Evangelistic Meetings being conducted in a Football Stadium in Cuba.

An open air Evangelistic Meeting conducted by Friedensstimme Mission in Russia.

THE MEMBERS OF STAFF - Back Row from the left : Billy French, Robin McCulla, Gary Bolton, Junior Hilland, Paul McGuiggan, Roger Lyons, Timothy Millen, David Senior, Ian De Courcy. Middle Row : Arthur Darragh, Stanley Watkins, Simon Wade, Gary Boal, Ernie McKeown, David Megarry, Douglas Condell, Stephen Roberts, Philip Hunter, Kenneth McCulla Front Row, Paul Allen, Heather Mercer, Clive Allen, Kathleen Allen, Ernie Allen, Carol Adams, Samuel Adams, Paul Roberts.

The pastor arranged an interview for Paul at Every Home Crusade. At that time there were no vacancies, but Samuel Adams assured Paul that his interest in the Crusade would be kept on file. The young man prayed that if the Lord wanted him into this work then He would open the door in due course. A short time later a phone call informed Paul that there was a position for him if he was still interested.

For seven years Paul has gleaned experience in various activities including folding and in the graphics department of the Crusade. He really enjoys being involved in helping to send the gospel all over the world. Paul said, "Besides enjoying my work, I have greatly benefited from working with other Christians who come from many different backgrounds. The highlight of the week for me is when we gather to pray on Monday mornings, and Samuel shares from the various letters which have arrived from abroad. It is then that we know our labour is not in vain in the Lord."

The 94th Boys Brigade company had a great influence in the life of young Billy French. After hearing a friend testify Billy attended the Jack Shuler Crusade at the Kings Hall in Belfast in the hot summer of 1955. The American evangelist preached with great power, and at the end of the meeting Billy accepted the Lord Jesus Christ as Saviour. That step not only changed his life, but set Billy on a course of service for Jesus Christ.

After accompanying a Child Evangelism Fellowship (CEF) outreach team to Lamorlaye in France in 1965, Billy enrolled the following year at the European Bible Institute to learn more of God's Word. He never felt that he would be a preacher, but he soon discovered that there were many other openings to serve the Lord as well as preaching in a pulpit. In 1969 he approached Sam Doherty, the European Director of CEF, who counselled Billy to pursue a course in the printing trade with a view of helping CEF with a planned printing programme.

He gleaned printing experience in various places, and after some time he was introduced to the work of Every Home Crusade and to Ernie Allen. At that time the Crusade was still occupying the premises at 285 Newtownards Road, and Billy worked with Ernie for a few months at the Crusade. Later he went to the CEF European Headquarters in Kilchzimmer, Switzerland, where he remained for twenty-three years, printing CEF material that was sent into Eastern Europe.

After the collapse of the Iron Curtain it became cheaper for CEF to print their materials in Eastern Europe rather than in Switzerland. With the print shop in Kilchzimmer redundant, it was suggested by the CEF leadership in 1995, that Billy consider returning to Belfast to work with the Every Home Crusade. For Billy this was a step he was happy to take for he had kept in touch with the progress of Every Home Crusade during the years he was absent from Northern Ireland.

With all the experience that Billy had gained in Switzerland, he was an asset to the team at Clara Street. On most days he is the first to arrive in the factory and has the machines rolling before 7:00 a.m. His colleagues jokingly say that Billy is such a workaholic, that if they could drip feed him by an intravenous drip he would work without a stop. Billy's defence is that he works hard because he loves his occupation. Furthermore, as he prints literature in various languages, he always remembers the man in Eastern Europe who introduced Billy to a group of believers with the moving comment, "Meet the man who printed books for us when under Communism we couldn't get any."

Ernie McKeown attends to correspondence for the Crusade from his home in Newtownabbey. Ernie became involved with Every Home Crusade in 1960 when he was part of a group of young men who committed themselves to placing gospel literature in every home in Enniskillen. He and his wife Evelyn maintained a practical and prayerful interest in Ernie Allen's work in the succeeding years as the Crusade began to grow.

In August 1986 Ernie had opportunity to visit Korea and see first hand some of the effects of the great revival with which that part of Asia had been greatly favoured. The visit made a deep impression on his life. At one of the large churches in Seoul, a mammoth text hung on the wall. Its bold letters seemed to burn into Ernie's eyes and soul, "Go ye into all the world..." He could not eliminate the words from his vision, nor the challenge from his soul. Immediately on return to Northern Ireland he approached Ernie Allen about working as a volunteer at the Crusade. Ernie was inducted into the work the following month.

His initial responsibilities were to attend to foreign mail. When letters arrive from abroad they are separated into different categories. Some are appeals for literature and these are processed into the appropriate department. However, there are many correspondents who inquire about the way of salvation. These letters require personal attention in addressing their questions and counselling them in the Lord. Ernie not only fulfilled this role, but he has found it to be most satisfying. His letters have even gone to many criminals on death row, who for obvious reasons were anxious about their spiritual welfare. He also corresponds with pastors, evangelists and people from all walks of life.

When Ernie McKeown installed a suitable word processor and labeller at his home, he moved his Crusade operation. Besides attending to foreign mail, he also addresses labels for those who request packs of literature. At regular intervals he travels to the Crusade offices and exchanges the prepared envelopes for more correspondence to attend to.

Here is a typical letter, retained as the correspondent wrote it, which gives an insight into Ernie McKeown's work.

> Dear Mister Allen,
>
> How can I find the right words to thank you for the booklet "Pardon for Sin and Assurance of Peace With God," which you sent to me with other gospel publications. Also I received the letter from Mister Ernie McKeown. Please tell to him my thanks. I learned very much about the way of salvation from your booklets, and about our Lord Jesus Christ. I do not want to serve Jesus Christ with half of my heart and part of myself and part of my possessions. I wanna say all for Him, all from the bottom of my heart.

I have made the decision I surrender myself unconditionally to His Lordship over me. I am thirty-five years old, and I may be able to serve Him long years more. My family are Roman Catholics, and they do not understand that "Neither is there salvation in any other. For there is none other name under heaven, given among men, whereby we must be saved." I know that our souls can be saved by Jesus only. Until now I thought my sins were too great and too serious to be forgiven. But I was wrong.

Dear Mr. William,

Thank you for showing me the correct way of salvation, which leads to Jesus Christ. I am amazed how many people cannot understand the true way. They are going to the wrong gate. All will not be saved and the majority will be lost. There is no hope beyond the grave. There is no second chance. My friend, may the Lord richly bless you. I am praying that you and Mister Ernie McKeown will do great service for our Jesus Christ - The Saviour. Your sincere friend.

Not every one who came to work at the Every Home Crusade made it their life's work. Many have arrived at vital stages and made a contribution to the work then moved on elsewhere. Each one's work is appreciated.

After retiring from the work of the Faith Mission, John and Emily Currie kept busy for the Lord by addressing envelopes and processing mail for Every Home Crusade. John invited his brother Herbie Currie to join them in their contribution. Herbie's inclusion had a strange touch of irony about it for he had been Samuel Adams' headmaster when Samuel was a pupil at Drumbo Primary School. Now he came to work under Sam's leadership. Herbie is a good friend of Ernie's and is a missionary-minded Christian.

Stanley Watkins, Arthur Darragh, Ken McCulla and Roger Lyons arrive every Tuesday to spend the day filling envelopes that Ernie McKeown prepared the previous week. Derek Shannon, Billy Johnson and John McDowell also gave much of their valuable time to preparing material to be sent to those who had requested literature.

Although the factory floor has always been the domain of men, throughout the years the Crusade has been greatly blessed by a succession of Christian ladies who dedicated their time and skills to work in the Crusade's offices. Mrs. Joan Owens (nee Trotter) from County Fermanagh completed her missionary training with the Independent Methodist College in Portrush, before coming to the Every home Crusade. She was of a quiet disposition but very efficient in her work as the Crusade's secretary for almost three years.

When Joan left to be married Lorna Harpur from near Omagh in County Tyrone stepped into the vacancy. Lorna had trained at the same College as Joan and for some time had worked as an Independent Methodist Church evangelist. Lorna served with the Crusade very proficiently in the office for a three year period until she transferred into another sphere of service for the Lord in the Child Evangelism Fellowship.

Other Christian volunteers came in for one day each week and render a service for their Lord in some aspect of the work. Time and space fail us to include everybody who played a part in the development and effectiveness of this ministry, but each one's contribution is appreciated. Men such as Jim Todd, David Harper and Paul Elliot gave faithful and valuable years of dedicated service in the print shop of the Every Home Crusade.

> There has been a lot of dedication and hard work through difficult times also. One young man who is a printer with the Crusade was offered a very profitable job working for the government. His respectful reply was, "I am printing for the King of Kings, and I am not going to step down to print for the Queen of England."

Letters coming from different continents encourage all members of the Crusade team to keep their eyes on the goal as they serve the Lord in the confines of the factory. They realise that around the world there are hundreds of millions of empty hands reaching out for God's Word and the gospel message.

"Death Row", Malawi

Dear Friend,

I am writing this letter to you to let you know that through reading your gospel booklets and tracts here in prison, which I received from Pastor Chikaonga, I have come to know the Lord Jesus Christ as Saviour in a way I would never have thought possible for me in my life. I do not have long to live before I will be executed, but I want you to know that I have now received strength and courage. I want to ask you to pray for me during this time.

Blantyre, Malawi

Dear Sir,

I want to thank you for the booklet, "Pardon and Assurance of Peace with God," which you sent to me along with other tracts and leaflets. I am happy now after trusting in Jesus Christ our Lord as my Saviour. I pray three times a day, and sometimes more when I am alone. I used to drink alcoholic drink, but now I have no more desire to drink. Many people are surprised to see me living my new life, and they ask me questions. I tell them the good news of the Lord Jesus and pray for them. I am asking you to send me some more Christian literature to help in our soul-winning ministry. May the Lord bless you in your work.

A thrilling testimony, Nigeria

Dear Mr. Allen,

I was travelling in a bus, and a gentleman gave me a copy of your gospel tract, "A Wicked Young Man Wishes to do Penance." I read the tract and reflected on my past life. In all honesty I felt that I was a worse sinner than that young man. As I read repeatedly over the tract, suddenly I became a different person. A new life seemed to run through my body, and the burden of my sins fell off.

Saved from going to Hell, Ghana

Dear Mr. Ernest,

I am glad to write you this letter. I am from a poor family, but I am a follower of the Lord Jesus Christ. Mr. Ernest, through the ministry of your gospel literature I have been saved from going to hell, because I read one of your Scripture booklets called, "The Way of Salvation Through Our Lord Jesus Christ." When I read it I knew I was a sinner. I confessed my sins and trusted in Jesus as my Saviour. In this booklet I found your address. I will never forget you.

Nearly derailed by Satan, now saved, Kenya

Dear Brother Allen,

Some time ago I wrote to you for the booklet "Pardon and Assurance", and you also sent me some gospel tracts. Satan did his best to derail me, but in December I could no longer spurn God's offer of pardon. Then I received the Lord Jesus as my Saviour, and it has been a joyful life ever since. I am at the University of Nairobi. During a vacation I have seen prayer answered, and we now have a fellowship of about ten born again Christians. Please send me more of your leaflets and gospel tracts for my spiritual growth.

A Life Transformed, Lagos

Dear Brother Allen,

Thank you for all thc publications which you sent to me. I thank God for the precious blood of Jesus that cleansed me from my sins and made me whole. I thank the Lord too for the souls that have been won to our Lord Jesus Christ through your literature. I put up some of your posters in an open place at my shop where everybody could see them. Many persons have been spoken to by the Lord through these posters, "The Way of the Cross Leads to Heaven" and "Don't Join the Losers." Through your gospel tracts you have brought the light of the Gospel into many dark homes. Please send me more of these tracts, leaflets and booklets. May the Lord continue and complete the ministry which He has given to you.

Coming to Know Jesus, Kenya

Dear Sir,

I thank the Lord whom you serve and whom I serve too. I came to know Jesus as my Saviour a few months ago. I was at home one day when my sister came from school with a gospel leaflet in her hand. She asked me to read it. I said "Sure," and read "A Royal Invitation - Jesus Says Come Unto Me." After I finished reading, I knelt down and asked the Lord to take away my heavy load of sin. Now I am rejoicing in the Lord. But, sir, I need your help. Please send me your booklet, "Pardon for Sin and Assurance of Peace with God".

A former Moslem, Toulouse, France

Dear Brother Allen,

I really thank the Lord for your gospel tract "A Moslem Governor's Questions." It has helped me a lot. I have been converted from the Moslem faith to the Christian faith. This tract is helping me and other Christian brothers in our witnessing for the Lord to other Moslems. Please send me more of your publications.

A nurse weeping seeking the Saviour, Nigeria

Dear Sir,

The first day I read your gospel tract "A Royal Invitation - Jesus Says Come Unto Me" I wept because before that time I had been to and fro searching for a god to help me. Sir, I have learned that there is only one Saviour, the Lord Jesus Christ. I want to know more about Him. Please send me a copy of your booklet "Pardon and Assurance", also some tracts which I will use to deliver people from the power of darkness to the Lord Jesus Christ. I am a nurse who works at a Maternal and Child Health Centre, so I hope to preach the gospel to the mothers who come here for care. I hope to hear from you soon and a big greeting for yourself.

A testimony, Zimbabwe

Dear Mr. Allen,

Thank you for the booklet "Pardon and Assurance" and the other literature you sent to me. I am pleased to know that Jesus died on the cross for my salvation. I was in the darkness of sin. I was like the chaff mentioned in one of your leaflets. I thank the Lord and you that I am now a true

Christian. I was living in a world of darkness, but now I am living in the light of God's holiness. I thank you for bringing me to our Saviour.

It must be clear to all that the printed page is mighty. When that page carries the message of the gospel of Jesus Christ it has the power to transform lives in every country. The team at Every Home Crusade works together in order for the Word to go forth.

Chapter Thirteen

Where Do We Go From Here?

A mushroom will grow overnight. Radishes grow in fourteen days. Redwood trees take over a thousand years to be fully grown. Behind all these is the hand and power of the mighty Creator who makes them all grow. The same Creator is responsible for the growth of the Every Home Crusade. In New Testament times the Apostle Paul recognised that while he may plant and another preacher may reap, it was God who made the harvest grow. God supplied the substantial needs of the Crusade. He blessed their ministry. He was working mightily through the printed page.

By 1989 the Redcar Street plant was operating at full capacity. Besides the folding and stitching machines, four presses were running constantly and producing millions of Scripture booklets, tracts and leaflets in one year.

The "Good News" report for December 1989 gave the following headline and summary:

Ninety-four Tonnes of Literature Printed in 1989

I am very pleased to share with you this good news that during the year with the blessing of the Lord and the support of our Christian friends together we have been enabled to see the work of the Every Home Crusade expand tremendously, as can be seen from the following details.

About sixty tonnes of the Scripture booklets were printed in twelve languages. Over ninety-four tonnes of paper were used during the year. The actual totals of all the publications printed are as follows:

- 10,701,750 gospel tracts.
- 1,259,000 gospel and revival leaflets.
- 4,832,000 gospel and Scripture booklets in 12 languages
- 846 tea chests full of literature were sent out.

These were distributed in the following way:

- 339 tea chests were sent to the Philippines.
- 246 were sent to African countries.
- 151 tea chests full of the Scripture booklets were sent to Russia.
- 50 were sent to South American countries
- 30 to other parts of the world.
- In addition, 3,827 large parcels of the literature were posted to many parts of the world including the British Isles.
- We are sending supplies of literature to over 50 countries of the world.
- 1,000,000 Scripture booklets in Russian were printed during the year.
- Hundreds of millions of people throughout the world are still without a word of the Scriptures. Pray for the Lord's enabling and guidance as we seek to print millions of the Scripture booklets in more languages for Russia, India, Poland, Africa and the Philippines.

Millions of powerful "printed missionaries" were sent forth in the Every Home Crusade. These printed missionaries give a true Scriptural message. They never show cowardice; never are tempted to compromise; they do not tire or grow disheartened, nor do they ever lose their temper; they are able to enter a home and stay there. These missionaries travel cheaply, and they require no hired building. As gospel preachers they can go anywhere, live without food and can tolerate all climates. They enter idol temples and can speak without an audible voice ever being heard. Their words have led millions of souls to the Saviour. The whole world is the parish of the printed page.

Besides these large amounts of literature being sent out, the Every Home Crusade attended to a request from the Cameroons to print a hymn book for believers. Calendars and Christmas cards were also printed and made available to the public in the British Isles.

The income for 1989 was in excess of £206,000, and ten men were working full-time on the factory floor. The increased production at the Redcar Street factory was an undoubted blessing to millions who received the literature, but it did present problems. The 3,000 square feet of floor space was inadequate for the demands that were now being made on production levels. The print shop could not house any more machinery. The storage area had been enlarged but was now too small. In the same December report an appeal was sent out to supporters of the work.

We have plans before the Belfast Council for permission to extend the premises here, in order to have space for more printing equipment to provide Scriptures to place in the millions of hands reaching out to us from around the world. Please continue to pray every day for much fruit that will remain for our Lord Jesus Christ.

This extension work was done by Stuart McCartney and his friends. The project was completed in May 1990. It was used to house another large German press which was installed on 18th June. It was able to produce 6,000 gospel booklets per hour. Every time the output of Scripture portions increased, the requests for more literature also increased.

During 1990, 25,000 seeking souls and young converts wrote to the Every Home Crusade either to report on their conversion or to ask for help. One hundred and forty tonnes of paper were used that year. Soon twelve tonnes of literature went out each month. The average bill to mail parcels abroad cost £5,000 per month. It seemed obvious to the leadership that the Lord was encouraging them to reach for still greater things.

Stanley Manus was always a great encouragement to the workers at the Every Home Crusade. Although the extension at Redcar Street gave some extra space, Stanley unceasingly insisted that the Every Home Crusade needed larger premises. Ernie listened to Stanley but thought that maybe down the road a bit he would have to consider a move. It came earlier than Ernie anticipated.

Within a year of the Redcar Street extension being completed, it became obvious that the Crusade had outgrown the converted school building which they had occupied for twelve years. They prayerfully began to look around. It was felt that the factory should remain in East Belfast, so a survey was made of the general area. Existing buildings that were available were very expensive to purchase. Besides, an existing building would have to be refurbished and adopted to the needs of the Crusade. Over a period of several months there was much prayer and discussion about the way ahead.

One day when Samuel drove up Clara Street, which is just a quarter of a mile from Redcar Street, he noticed a large sign advertising a vacant site at the rear of a new development of houses. The blurb on the large wooden sign indicated the site was twelve thousand square feet and was zoned for six light industrial units. Samuel parked the car to take a look at the site. There were two old garages on the lot and a high fence cordoned off the rest of the area. As Samuel was looking around and considering the various possibilities a large bone was flung over a yard wall and hit Samuel in the middle of his back. He was not sure if this was a slap on the back to encourage him to positively proceed or a thump to warn him to clear off.

Enquiries revealed that the site had been on the market previously. Apparently a closure had been made, but this had fallen through, and now it was available again. Ernie and Samuel discussed the potential of the site which offered three times the capacity of the Redcar Street factory. They were aware of the need for expansion but carried the responsibility of being wise stewards of the Lord's treasury. The more they prayed about the matter the more they sensed that this was the Lord's place. It offered the space they needed, in the locality they wanted and the planning permission was already granted. There was one more formidable hurdle, the owner was asking £38,000 for the site. The prompting to make an offer for the site was confirmed in a remarkable way.

George and Vinny Hamilton of Enniskillen had been trustworthy friends and supporters of the Every Home Crusade for many years. George worked for the Northern Ireland Electricity Board. He was also the leader of the Irish Evangelistic Band's Hall in Enniskillen. He led the first group of workers who engaged in placing the Crusade literature in every home in County Fermanagh in 1960. He also made frequent visits to the Irish Republic to distribute literature in towns and villages. Sadly, George became the casualty of a terminal illness which took his life in 1989. Two weeks later his wife, Vinny, also died of the same disease. Their deaths were a devastating blow for their extended family and their friends in Christian work.

Denzil McIlfatrick, George's brother-in-law and close friend, was the executor of the couple's will. He phoned Ernie Allen to inform him that the Hamiltons' home had been left to the Every Home Crusade. Ernie and Samuel had no prior knowledge of this large legacy to the Crusade, but they felt it was more than coincidental that the value of the property bequeathed to the Crusade amounted to £37,000 which was adequate to purchase the site for the new home for the Every Home Crusade. With money in hand the Crusade was able to negotiate the purchase of the site for £33,000.

Architect David Watson was impressed by the site and consented to draw the plans for the new printing plant. These were submitted to the appropriate building authorities and accepted in September 1991. Four building firms were invited to tender for the contract to build the unit. All these steps were bathed in prayer. A friend of the Crusade had recommended Greer Morrison, a Christian contractor from Dromara, as a dependable and responsible builder with very competitive pricing.

In the May edition of the "Good News" report, news of the new project was shared with friends and supporters of the work

Important Announcement:

Planning to Build a Larger Gospel Literature Factory

The work of the Every Home Crusade is growing week by week, and the requests for the literature continue to pour in from more than fifty countries of the world. For some time we have realised that we need much larger premises in order to carry on this worldwide gospel literature ministry efficiently. Now a suitable site of almost 12,000 square feet has become available, and we have come to an agreement with the owners about the price to be paid. Plans are being prepared for the building of new premises of about 10,500 square feet.

Samuel was taking part in a Child Evangelism Fellowship Camp when he received a phone call from Greer submitting his price for the job. His proposal was far lower than the other prices submitted. David Watson, the architect, felt there must have been a mistake in the costing so he invited Greer and Samuel to his office on the Ormeau Road in Belfast to verify the price. At the end of this meeting the three men were all satisfied that the price submitted was satisfactory, and Greer's submission was accepted.

When the construction got under way there were many contractors and friends who rallied to provide materials and finance to help in the construction. The leadership at the Crusade had been alerted to the security situation prevailing in East Belfast. They prayed about this matter and felt constrained to display a large notice board at the building site indicating the purpose of the new building and giving prominence to the name of the Crusade and a large gospel text. During the six months period of building there was neither threat to the Crusade, nor intimidation to the building contractor. God had His protecting Hand on the work.

After the foundation was laid Walter Watson, a Christian contractor from Castlewellan, was contracted to construct the steel for the outer frame of the building. Bricklayers, joiners, plumbers and electricians all worked under the supervision of Greer Morrison who confessed that building the new unit was one of the most unusual experiences he ever had in the building trade. Every time he brought an invoice to Ernie Allen the bill was paid the very same day. As contractor for the unit he acknowledged that he not only built the factory, but the experience built him up in his faith. "I grew more spiritually during those months than at any other time in my Christian life. Mr. Allen came to the site every day and prayed with me on the job. For me it was an honour to work with the leadership of the Crusade."

During the months of the construction, the members of the Crusade staff kept busy at their work producing the literature at the usual pace in Redcar Street. They marvelled to see the Lord supply, not only the needs for the everyday running of the Crusade's printing programme, but the additional needs to pay for the new building also.

One morning an envelope arrived in the post with a £20,000 cheque from an anonymous donor. On another day a lady arrived and handed Ernie a brown paper bag. He thanked the sister for her gift without knowing what was in the bag. He opened it in the privacy of his office and discovered it contained one thousand £5 notes that had obviously been stored at home. Other gifts were not just so substantial, but were none-the-less sacrificial for those who gave to the Lord's work. The total price of the new unit was £190,000. The income for 1991 amounted to £314,656.

Week by week the construction progressed towards completion. Often businessmen would stop and enquire what the new unit would be used for. One local preacher announced that it was big enough to be an aircraft hangar. The completion date was eagerly anticipated by all. Never at any time did the Crusade have to go into debt, or incur an overdraft in the bank to finance the building of the new factory in Clara Street.

The building was finally opened to the glory of God on Saturday, 11th April, 1992. Seven hundred people attended two conference services to mark the opening of the Gospel Literature Factory. Pastor S. T. Carson from Banbridge Baptist Church opened and dedicated the building to the work of the gospel and the glory of God. Pastor Noel Darragh of Straid Congregational Church was the guest preacher. There was a full supporting programme of testimonies from team members and bright singing. It was a memorable day of praise and thanksgiving. The free-will offering totaled over £23,000 which was an expression of the supporters' confidence in the ministry of the Crusade. Refreshments were provided between the two conference meetings.

On the day of the opening there was an unveiling of two plaques in the entrance hall of the new complex. One was in memory of Frederick Starrett, the former colleague at Every Home Crusade who had been assassinated by IRA terrorists in 1988. The other was in memory of George and Vinny Hamilton whose generous legacy provided the money to purchase the site of the new Gospel Literature Factory. They were not aware of plans to construct a new factory when they allocated the sale of their home to the Crusade after their decease, but they followed the Lord's instruction, and He worked out the details.

The literature production was suspended for less than a week to allow for the transfer of the equipment and machinery to the new building. Once the presses, collating, folding and stitching machines were set in place full production started again. Over the next month a record 123 tonnes of literature were sent out from the new Gospel Literature Factory. The new store allowed the Crusade to receive fifty tonnes of paper in one delivery.

There was minimum interruption in other departments of the work which moved into newly equipped offices. During the month in which they transferred to Clara Street 2,020 letters arrived from seeking souls and new converts at the Crusade's office. In one day alone 506 letters arrived from abroad.

As soon as the Crusade team settled into their new surroundings the leadership of the Crusade decided to send out an invitation to their local supporters.

An Invitation to Visitors

Since the opening of this new Gospel Literature Factory some of our friends have brought groups of Christians from their church, prayer meeting, mission hall, or ladies' meeting to see the factory with the printing machines operating and the packing of the literature. If you wish to arrange such a visit during the day or an evening, please contact us so that we can arrange a suitable date and time. You and your friends will be more than welcome.

Very soon groups of Christians from all over Northern Ireland made special excursions to the factory and enjoyed a conducted tour of the new premises with the factory in full operation. Supper was provided after the tour. These visits deepened people's interest and understanding of the work and greatly enhanced the support base for the ministry. Quarterly conferences were also convened on Saturday afternoons at the factory. For these the factory floor was reorganised to accommodate two hundred people. Missionaries returning from abroad and local pastors and evangelists took part in these conferences.

Corresponding with the time of moving into Clara Street, the leadership of the Crusade took another big step of faith to trust God to provide the funds to purchase a new Heidelberg Sormz. This was one of the company's top quality and most efficient printing presses which cost £120,000 in 1992. This press was able to print 8,000 sheets of print in two colours per hour, and the sheet sizes were double the size of those fed into all the other presses.

The Redcar Street property was sold to a church group for £40,000 and this money helped offset some of the cost of the new machine. Other gifts came in to complete the total for the payment of the machine. The Crusade was very happy to make the purchase.

However, there was a hiccup in the delivery process. Early in the month of October 1992 the Heidelberg Company sent word to say that this seven tonne printing machine could be installed by their technicians on Monday 21st October, 1992. Nearer to the delivery date the company phoned again to say there was a slight delay, and they wanted to postpone the installation of the new press until Wednesday the 23rd. The date of delivery was significant because the international financial transaction between supplier and purchaser was to be completed on the day the machine is installed and with the exchange rates the price could vary from day to day. On the day prior to the new date earmarked for the installation of the press, Samuel received a phone call from the Heidelberg agent to inform him that there had been a collapse of the Pound Sterling against the Deutsche Mark on the previous day. Monday 21st October 1992 was known as "Black Monday" on the London Stock Market. As a result, Heidelberg had to increase the price of the machine by an extra £10,000. This left the Crusade in a dilemma. They had never failed to honour their financial commitments on time, but now they were presented with a large increase on the price of the new machine, and this left them bewildered to know what to do.

Just at that moment it seemed that the Lord prompted Samuel to point out to the Heidelberg agent that the supplier had initially indicated that the machine would be installed on Monday 21st October and the subsequent delay which was arranged at their behest, resulted in the increase in price. It now was the turn of the agent to be bewildered. He reported the dilemma back to his headquarters. Heidelberg finally agreed to forgo the increased tariff and reverted to the original price. The Lord was in control of every detail.

This new addition to the factory brought the number of presses operating every day to six. Machines producing such a volume of literature meant that other equipment had to be updated so that there would not be a bottle neck to hold up the production line. A new folding machine was purchased at £40,000. Furnishing this factory with the needed machinery involved giant steps of faith. The price of the new printer and the folding machine was almost equal to the total price of the new building. The Lord gave the vision to enlarge and increase, and He provided the means for the Crusade to take those steps.

Chapter Fourteen

TRUTH TRAVELS FAR

The world seems to have shrunken considerably in the fifty years since Ernie embarked on his literature Crusade. The "slow boat to China" concept of travel has been transformed in class, cost and speed. There are few parts of our globe that cannot be reached in less than twenty-four hours. What used to be considered as distant mission fields, do not seem to be so far away.

For all the change and improvement in travel Ernie Allen is not known as an international leader who has travelled the world promoting the cause of the movement he founded. Like his Lord who left his native Palestine on only one occasion during the years of His ministry, Ernie left the British Isles on only one occasion to attend a short conference in Paris and that merely for a few days. However, the gospel in printed form sent from the Every Home Crusade has circumnavigated the globe countless times. Ernie Allen's name, like that of the Every Home Crusade, is known on all continents.

One Sunday after a deputation meeting for the Every Home Crusade, Samuel Adams and his family were invited for a meal with a Christian family. During the general conversation over the meal the host family suggested to Samuel that in view of the growth of the Crusade's work he should think of going to visit some of these fields. Several months earlier Samuel had considered this idea himself and prayed about the matter. He found no particular leading and dismissed the idea from his thoughts for the meantime.

Samuel was aware that Mr. Allen was not a traveller, and therefore it seemed most unlikely that he would travel abroad. One week later Ernie invited Samuel into his office and said he had a call from a Christian man who suggested that it might be a good idea for Samuel to visit Kenya and Zaire (now the Democratic Republic of the Congo), two of the Crusade's target fields. Ernie told Samuel if he was willing to go, then the friend who phoned would pay the price of the fare. As they talked it over Ernie encouraged Samuel to make the trip and see first hand what the Lord was doing in that part of Africa. Every Home Crusade had sent millions of Scripture booklets to Kenya, Zaire and many other African countries.

They discussed the matter and decided that rather than Samuel travel alone, it would be a good idea to invite Eric Magowan to go with him. Eric and his wife had been missionaries in Zaire and Kenya for many years. His knowledge of the country and language would be a great asset during the trip.

Samuel and Eric set out for Zaire in April 1996. Samuel gave an account of their experience.

> The city of Nairobi has a population of two million people. It is a city of contrasts. There are large office blocks and beautiful homes where wealthy people live, while the majority live in terrible poverty.
>
> My first day was spent in the Soweto slum. As we walked with the local Christians through the slum and viewed the wooden and tin shacks which are home to thousands of

people, we could see and smell the results of no running water or sewage system in this district.

Far worse than the social misery, is the spiritual condition in which these people are living. The powers of darkness are evident, and many know nothing of the love of our Lord Jesus Christ in their lives. However, it was encouraging to see both young and old alike keen to receive copies of the Scripture booklet "The Way of Salvation Through our Lord Jesus Christ" in a variety of languages.

As a result of the evangelistic outreach of a small church in Soweto many souls have been saved, and these new Christians are slowly leaving this slum area and returning to their home villages. The new converts carry their faith with them and are now opening small churches in their villages.

We left Kenya and flew to Zaire where we visited the headquarters of Diguna, an evangelical German Mission working in Zaire. They use large lorries to transport teams of young German Christians over the extremely bad and treacherous roads to reach the region which they wish to evangelise. In these areas they collect the local pastors and evangelists and take them to preach the Gospel in the villages within their own area.

The Diguna teams provide loud-speaking equipment and have supplies of our gospel literature for distribution to the people who attend the meetings. I was very impressed with the vision and dedication of these teams of young Christians. During my visit a total of nine teams were working in different parts of Zaire, with at least one team being on the road for over three months.

Scripture booklets and gospel tracts are considered to be very valuable and are distributed with extreme care due to their scarcity. Each pastor may be given only thirty booklets for distribution in a day during which they will conduct seven open-air meetings.

Mr. Kurt Zander is one of the leaders of the Diguna Mission in Zaire. As I discussed with him the literature needs of the Diguna workers I realised that we need to send them a full eighteen tonne container load of tracts, leaflets and booklets.

We were very pleased to visit Miss Maizie Smyth in Kisangani. Conditions in Zaire are very difficult with extreme poverty everywhere. Most people can afford only two meals per day. As we stayed with Maizie we noticed that there was a constant stream of people visiting her - pastors, evangelists, young and old, all wanting to share with her their own particular problems.

Maizie showed real compassion, love and concern as she patiently listened, counselled and helped these people. We visited a Bible school where every home and classroom is built with sticks, mud and grass. The students have only a handful of study books. These students have felt the call of God upon their lives and want to study to become pastors to their own people.

After travelling forty miles on dirt roads, Maizie teaches two days a week in the Banjawade Bible School. It is thrilling to see the spirituality and humility in the lives of these students. One of the men whom we met had been a local government official. When he got saved he had thirteen wives. For a time he prayed about this situation until, one by one his wives left him. Now he is in Bible school with one wife.

On Sunday we attended church and were thrilled to see five-to-six hundred people in attendance. Sadly, we noticed there were hardly any hymn books available for the people during the church services. This is a common problem in most of the churches.

Maizie told us that in some village churches if the pastor is away for any reason they simply cancel the Sunday Service, as no one else has got a copy of the Bible. As I discussed the needs for evangelistic literature with the head of the Evangelism Department at the Bible school I asked, "How long will it take to distribute the literature which you have at present?"

He replied, "We could distribute it all in one day, as the people are so eager to receive it. However, we are very careful how we distribute the booklets and tracts, as we do not know how long it will be until we receive another supply of literature."

At present Maizie, with the help of a Bible school teacher, is translating more tracts and the booklet "Pardon and Assurance" into the Lingala language. When this is completed we will print and send another eighteen tonne container load of literature to Maizie in Kisangani.

In Nairobi I visited the various headquarters of some mission agencies and church groups which have a total of about seven thousand churches in their care across Kenya. I heard the same message time after time. "We have no tracts or anything like these Scripture booklets." "We don't have tracts, they are far too expensive." "Pastors constantly come to us for supplies of tracts, but we don't have any to give to them."

When I explained that we would be willing to send to them large supplies of our tracts, leaflets and booklets completely free of charge, I was told in a very excited manner, "We wish we had known about your literature ministry years ago. You have brought great joy to our hearts today. Please send immediately 300,000 Scripture booklets in English, Swahili, Kamba, Kikuyu and Luo."

Mr. Ed Morrow who received our containers of literature in Nairobi and distributed consignments to many missionaries, gave us lists of requests which had been received from pastors and evangelists who had come to him for supplies of gospel literature.

We attended an open air meeting in the centre of Nairobi. Hundreds of people including the street children stopped and listened to the gospel message being preached. At the end of the meeting a very short appeal was made, and about twenty people came forward professing to accept Jesus Christ to be their Saviour.

Hundreds of Scripture booklets were then distributed by four men, but they could not move as people simply surrounded them. Hundreds were reaching out with empty hands, all trying to obtain a booklet before the supply was exhausted. Not one booklet was dropped on the ground.

On my last Sunday morning I quickly visited about five churches in Nairobi in order to see as much as I could in the limited time. I was thrilled to see large churches seating over one thousand people; many others sat outside. Some of these churches have three services starting early on Sunday morning. Even with churches full the streets were crammed with people still to be reached with the gospel message.

As I looked at the masses of people in Kenya and Zaire, I realised these must be reached with the Gospel message urgently, so that they may receive "the gift of God which is eternal life through Jesus Christ our Lord." This is why we are going to send a further eighteen tonnes of tracts, leaflets and booklets to Kenya as soon as possible.

Since Samuel and Eric returned from that trip, the Democratic Republic of Congo has been ravished with strife and civil war. Many believers have been killed or have fled their homes to take refuge in the forests. Missionaries were forced to withdraw from the country, and as a result of the war it has not been possible to send any literature to that troubled country. It is most unlikely these believers have any literature left.

There are many tribal languages in Africa, and the Crusade depends on nationals or missionaries to give good translations of the various Every Home Crusade publications. One of these translators, Patrick Moroto, works from Kenya in an endeavour to reach his own people in the Sudan. The Crusade published an account of his work in the "Good News" newsletter.

> Patrick Moroto lives in Nairobi and has translated the Scripture booklets "The Way of Salvation" and the "Gospel of John - Seven Steps to Knowing God" into the Bari, Moru, Dinka , Lotuko and Nuer languages of Sudan. During May we requested Miss Maizie Smyth to take some copies to Patrick Moroto for checking, while she was working in Nairobi, Kenya. She wrote the following article.
>
> I visited Patrick Moroto on 24th May. I called at his office which is part of his home on the third floor of a very, very dark building in the midst of a market slum area of Nairobi. A young girl was typing for him in a very poorly equipped office.
>
> He gave me a resume of his life. Patrick was born as a healthy child in a church family in Sudan. When he was nine years old he contracted polio which stunted his growth and has left him paralysed, so that he cannot move without his two crutches. As a teenager he watched the lives of the Christians around him, and then he too accepted the Lord Jesus Christ.
>
> He was pleased to be gifted in languages, but due to the war in Sudan he came to Nairobi for work. While in Nairobi he became very ill, almost to the point of death. He realised that he did not want to spend his whole life translating secular material. Couldn't he do something to help the people in Sudan read God's Word? Today he has finished checking the "Way of Salvation" and "The Gospel of John" in the Bari language.

There are two million Bari people, many of whom do not have God's Word in their hands. He hopes to be able to shortly return to Sudan. He said, "I only want to tell my people in Sudan the wonderful news of my lovely Saviour."

Patrick is requesting Every Home Crusade to send over 200,000 "Gospel of John" and Scripture booklets to Sudan so that he can supply these to churches and the Sudanese evangelists.

In the work to the Philippines the Crusade appreciates the work of Chetan Pribhdas, a forty-six year old Filipino who was converted after he accepted a "Gospel of John" booklet on a street in Manila. After reading the contents he came to personal faith in Jesus Christ. After his conversion he dedicated his life to engage in the same activity that brought him to Jesus Christ and be a distributor of gospel literature.

Eventually he was able to make contact with the Every Home Crusade in Belfast and requested a supply of their booklets and tracts to use in his city. Very soon he was receiving parcels of gospel literature for other groups in the Philippines. This distribution developed greatly until the Crusade was shipping hundreds of tea chests of the gospel literature to Chetan's address.

He often received up to sixty tea chests of gospel literature in various languages at one time from the Crusade. He stored them in his small apartment. From his flat he distributed the boxes and parcels to pastors and churches all over the country.

The increasing demands for the Every Home Crusade literature in the Philippines made it impossible for Chetan to store the volume of material being shipped to Manila. A depot of some sort was needed to receive at least an eighteen tonne container. With this in view, Ernie encouraged Samuel to visit the Philippines. Accordingly they wrote to Chetan and suggested the plan for Samuel to go to Manila on the 9th-23rd April, 1998 to appraise the situation and explore the possibility of finding a warehouse to receive the increasing supplies of literature.

Before Chetan replied to the letter Samuel received a telephone call from Manila. The person on the other end introduced himself as James Tioco. Chetan had shown Samuel's letter to James, and he decided to take the matter into his own hands. He discussed the strategy of literature distribution in the Philippines. After fifteen minutes on the phone James invited Samuel come to Manila, and he would arrange a full itinerary for him there.

Unknown to Samuel at the time James was a vital contact. He was a zealous thirty-five year old Christian and the owner of a telecommunication company in Manila with five hundred workers in his employment. His offices and warehouses had all the infrastructure needed to handle the import of large quantities of literature. James was at the time the national treasurer of the Gideons International and is currently the Vice President of that organisation. Obviously, he is a very well known and greatly respected man all over the Philippines. The Lord had guided them to the right man.

James took precious time away from his business responsibilities to accompany Samuel during the two weeks he visited Manila. On his return from Manila, Samuel wrote this report.

> Brother James Tioco arranged my programme of meetings and interviews with Christian leaders. He did a tremendous job, and I am very grateful to him and his wife for all their help and fellowship. James is a businessman with a large staff. I was very much impressed with his evident love for our Lord Jesus Christ and his deep concern for the salvation of the people of the Philippines.
>
> We are delighted to know that he is willing to receive our containers of literature in his warehouse and is prepared to use his company to help in the distribution of the literature

to the many friends who are engaged in evangelism and soul-winning throughout the country.

Manila has a population of nine million people. The city has a vibrant business community, but there are also many thousands of people who live in absolute poverty.

I attended a Sunday open-air service of the Jesus is Lord Fellowship in Manila. There were ten thousand people at the meeting which is beamed out on television each Sunday evening. This Fellowship commenced about eighteen years ago as a Bible study in a university and has grown until now there are over one million members in churches in many parts of the Philippines. Brother Eddie Villanueva was the founder and is the leader of the Jesus is Lord Fellowship.

We visited a campsite where a conference was being conducted for pastors and Christian workers. There were about 1,300 Christians present. I told Eddie Villanueva about our publishing ministry and about the printing of the Gospel of John in Tagalog and Cebuano, about the Scripture booklets, and about the gospel tracts and leaflets. He told me that they had a tremendous need for large supplies of these publications and that they could use one million or more of our publications right away.

Brother Eddie told the friends present about our work and that we were going to send them supplies of our publications. As he told the people that we would be supplying them with our literature I was amazed to see the whole company breaking out into spontaneous applause just to show their appreciation. He then asked me to come and speak to the people. It was a very humbling experience to have that opportunity and to feel their interest and appreciation.

There are over 700 islands in the Philippines. In recent years there has been a moving of the Holy Spirit in the country. Multitudes have been turning to our Lord Jesus

Christ as Saviour. About twenty years ago it was estimated that there were 4,000 evangelical churches in the Philippines. Today there are about 32,000 evangelical churches throughout the country. The population of the Philippines is above seventy million people, eighty per cent of whom are Roman Catholic; fifteen per cent are Moslem, and five percent are Christian.

On the first Saturday evening in Manila, I went to see a Roman Catholic open-air meeting. It is estimated that nearly one million people gather for this meeting each week.

During our visit to Cebu City we were able to visit two prisons with Les Tilka, who works with the Christian Light Foundation. In these prisons I had the opportunity to take part in the meetings which were conducted for the prisoners. On both occasions about 100 prisoners sat listening with complete attention to the gospel message. It was a joy to see some of these prisoners who have trusted Jesus Christ as Saviour taking part in the meeting.

In Manila I was also able to see at first hand the work of Judy Russell who founded the Christian Light Foundation. She took me for a walk through one of the many slum areas in the city. Thousands of people live in absolute squalor and poverty. Judy has a health clinic for these people, and I was requested to share the gospel with everyone who was present at the clinic.

In our monthly reports we have quoted letters from Mrs. Valesco of Master Resources Ministries. These friends receive large quantities of literature from us and distribute it to pastors. Approximately 125 pastors come each month looking for literature from her. Because the supplies have been so small she frequently has no literature to pass on to them.

Among the many churches I visited were the Bible Baptist Churches of the Philippines. These friends have almost 300 churches in the southern part of the country.

> We visited one of the churches which seated about 5,000 people. On each side of the pulpit there was a large painting and on it the words "Go ye therefore..." To me this summed up the attitude of the Christians in the Philippines. They have a great desire to spread the good news of the gospel of our Lord Jesus Christ. Not only are they reaching their own people, but many Filipino Christians are now taking the gospel message to the multitudes in other Asian countries.

This visit was encouraging and enlightening for Samuel to see the results of the work first hand. The workers at the Crusade work hand-in-hand with fellow believers in distant lands. Every six months the Every Home Crusade sends a container full of gospel literature to James Tioco in Manila. Chetan Pribhdas still works with James, and they send the literature out to the various groups who are committed to evangelise the whole of the Philippines. Letters from the Bible Baptist Association in Cebu indicate how much God is blessing this work.

> Dear Brother Adams,
>
> This week we received the large consignment of 188 boxes of literature which you had sent to us. The Lord remains perfect in His timing because this coming week will be our Third World Mission's Conference. Our pastors from the provinces will be coming so we will distribute the 135 boxes of Gospels of John in the Cebanuo language to them. This will mean that 135 churches around the islands will be blessed with the opportunity to distribute these Gospels of John to our people. The Lord has brought the ministry of Every Home Crusade into our midst for such a time as this which has been a wonderful blessing. What a joy to be partners with you.

Another letter indicates the blessings.

Dear Brother Allen,

I received your letter and the booklet "Pardon and Assurance" plus leaflets and gospel tracts. All these helped me to seek our Lord Jesus for the forgiveness of my sins. Now I accept Him as my only personal Saviour, my Master and my King who will control my life. I have committed myself to Him saying, "All for Jesus." The tracts helped me a lot. I did not know that there is eternal punishment. I did not know that if I died unsaved my state would be fixed, and that I would suffer eternal punishment. Thank you for feeding me spiritually in Jesus' name. I believe you are working to save more souls. How I nearly lost my soul! Now I want you to send me some leaflets and tracts for distribution. This will be my first step in serving our Lord Jesus Christ. Praise the Lord!

Your brother in Christ,
Augelus

As well as Samuel being able to visit Africa and Asia, many missionaries, national pastors, evangelists and other contacts have been able to visit the Gospel Literature Factory in Belfast. This not only gives them an opportunity to see the production of the literature, but it also gives opportunity for those who supply the good Seed and those who distribute the Seed of God's Word to experience sweet fellowship with their co-workers in the gospel of Jesus Christ. Together they rejoice in the harvest where God gives the increase.

Chapter Fifteen

Publishing the Word for the World

In the Northern Hemisphere September is the time for the harvest season. Fields of waving corn and golden sheaves adorn the countryside. The apple orchards blush with the ripeness of their fruit. Farmers are busy taking advantage of any dry days to bring in the barley and wheat before winter sets in. The impending darkness gives an urgency to make sure all the harvest is gathered.

Likewise the harvest of reaching souls is urgent. The longer the church delays the longer the harvest will be neglected. The destiny of men and women is being decided. It is important that Christian reapers be busy while it is day for the time is coming when it will be too late to bring in the harvest of precious souls.

Ernie Allen has known this urgency in his mission work for fifty years. Even at eighty years of age, he is still busy every day at the factory, making sure that the good seed of the Word of God is sent out to the hungry souls that are waiting for it. The incoming letters tell of the reaping and of bringing in the sheaves in other lands. These letters encourage Ernie and the team to plan for the future. Some developments are prayerfully planned at the Crusade's office, while others come about without human planning.

India

There was little human planning involved when Mr. Maxton, leader of an organisation called Every Home for Christ in India, arrived in Northern Ireland for a series of meetings with a church group. His visit became a casualty of human error. He arrived to find no meetings had been arranged for him. Being summer time, it was the least opportune season for deputation meetings. Mr. Maxton did not know that there was an Every Home Crusade Gospel Literature Factory in Northern Ireland. Consequently, he did not know of Ernie or any of the workers, nor did they know him or of the work of Every Home for Christ.

A friend of Every Home Crusade took Mr. Maxton to visit the Gospel Literature Factory in Clara Street, where he was introduced to Ernie and Samuel. They were greatly touched as they listened to their colleague from India tell of the great need in his country. They had little or no resources, and their literature stocks were very low at that time. He explained to his new friends at Clara Street that he worked with 600 evangelists who distributed literature which was sent out from his depot in Secunderabad, but he had precious little to give them.

Mr. Maxton's face glowed when Ernie and Samuel readily promised to send literature from their factory to Every Home for Christ in India on a regular basis. His visit had been frustrated by a lack of meetings, but he received great encouragement in learning his literature depot would be replenished.

Since then the Crusade has been sending regular supplies to Every Home for Christ in India. One year after they started to supply gospel leaflets for Mr. Maxton the Indian government levied a heavy duty on all leaflets entering the country. Booklets, however, were exempt from this import tax. Samuel was able to redesign the leaflet and send the same literature in booklet form.

This newly designed booklet satisfied the authorities and allowed the distribution of the gospel literature to continue.

Mr. Maxton sent a report to the Crusade in November 1997 telling them of God's work in India.

Dear Brother Adams and Friends of Revival Movement Association,

Herewith I am sending you a brief report of our work during the past year. Multitudes of persons have been blessed in our country through your regular supply of Scripture booklets and other gospel publications in different languages. We are very grateful to you for your free and freight paid supplies of the literature.

Without your help it would be absolutely impossible for us to achieve the goals of our ministry. With the blessing of the Lord, our missionaries visited 1,824,174 homes distributing the gospel literature, and explaining the way of salvation. Over 2,720,000 Scripture booklets and gospel leaflets for adults and children were distributed. Personal conversations were entered into with many persons who wished to know more about the way of salvation.

Out of the multitudes who were dealt with personally and as the result of the Lord's blessing on our follow-up ministry, 113,559 persons clearly witnessed their faith in the Lord Jesus Christ by open confession of Him as Saviour. These young converts are now witnessing for Christ, and they meet together for Bible study and for Christian fellowship.

We praise the Lord that we have seen over 4,000 small church groups formed. This means that an average of over ten church groups have been formed every day during the past year. Praise the Lord! It is marvellous in our eyes to see these Christian groups now meeting in villages and

> other places where previously there was no Christian witness.
>
> From M. Maxton,
> Every Home for Christ, India.

Another unplanned development for the work in India was in meeting Dr. William Scott He was from Belfast and went to India as a missionary over forty years ago. He and his wife Joyce who is from the United States, founded the India Bible Literature Mission. During a visit to Northern Ireland Miss Elizabeth Hill, a friend of the Every Home Crusade, took Dr. Scott on a visit to the Gospel Literature Factory in Clara Street and encouraged Ernie to help the India Bible Literature Mission in their work. Dr. Scott was pleasantly surprised to learn what the Crusade was doing in many countries. He shared with Ernie and Samuel the burden on his heart for India and the work he and his wife were engaged in. After many years of difficult work when no one would join them in the distribution of the Scriptures, the Lord provided a team of one thousand and twenty evangelists who worked with the India Bible Literature Mission in the distribution of the Word of God.

He explained how the India Bible Literature Mission operates through so many evangelists.

> The India Bible Literature Mission operates a school of evangelism to which churches nominate Christian workers, or evangelists, who are already working for their own church to be enrolled in the School for one year. These students move from their own church and join a group of twelve evangelists who are designated to an unevangelised district of India where there is no church.
>
> The first month is spent in study and prayer following the India Bible Literature Mission School of Evangelism Course. At the end of one month each evangelist is appointed to visit one thousand homes over a period of the next three months. During this time they will distribute

Gospels of John, Scripture booklets "The Way of Salvation", "Who is Jesus?" and "The Guide to Happiness." These visits to homes are not short. Often the evangelist can spend at least an hour with each family explaining the gospel message to the people.

Later the students come together again for a further month of study. On average there will be around one hundred homes where people have responded to the distribution of the Scriptures and wish to know more about the gospel message. For the following few months these evangelists spend time explaining the gospel to these people, pointing men, women and young people to the Lord Jesus Christ as their Saviour.

At present there are eighty-five School of Evangelism groups operating in eighteen states in India which means that there are one thousand and twenty evangelists distributing literature and seeing a harvest of precious souls coming to the Lord Jesus Christ as their Saviour.

Dr. Scott agreed to become a distributor for the Every Home Crusade from their mission depot in Madras. They not only supply their own evangelists with the gospel material, but they also send it to other evangelistic groups throughout India. When the first supplies of literature arrived from Belfast the Indian Customs and Excise Authority impounded the eight tea chests and levied a very heavy duty to be paid to release the literature. The India Bible Literature Mission refused to pay the large amount of money.

The tonne of literature remained in the custody of the Customs until they decided to auction all unredeemed parcels and boxes. Dr. Scott and friends of the India Bible Literature Mission attended the auction and were able to purchase all the consignment at a greatly reduced cost than if they had paid what the customs had demanded. Since then the Every Home Crusade and the India Bible Literature Mission have been able to streamline their operation so that today the shipments are released with the minimum delay and expense.

Periodically Dr. Scott visits the Every Home Crusade factory in Belfast, and he is a regular correspondent with Ernie and Samuel. He sent a report soon after the first eighteen tonne containers arrived in Madras.

Dear Brother Adams,

India Bible Literature Mission's Management Committee takes this opportunity to thank you and your dedicated members who have been untiringly working and have made it possible for us to receive millions of copies of the Gospel of John, the Scripture and gospel booklets.

The blessings we are seeing today in the Lord's work in India commenced in the 1970s. At that time we did not have to go out to distribute the gospel literature to the people. The people were coming to us for the Scriptures. Their demand was greater than we could supply. In the 1980s this growth accelerated, and now that we are in the '90s we are living in a time of God's visitation in India.

God by His Spirit is moving on the Indian people, and many are coming to accept the Lord Jesus Christ as their personal Saviour. I used to go out evangelising alone or bring a school boy with me because there was not even one evangelist to go. What a difference from that time until today. The Lord has raised up and anointed thousands of evangelists and Bible women in India and has equipped them to do the work of the gospel. The Lord has done more in twenty years than what man could do in two hundred years, for He has now opened up the second most populous nation in the world to the gospel. India has a population of almost one billion people, and we have an opportunity now to give the gospel to this country in such a way as I never dreamed I would live to see.

We are very grateful to you in the Every Home Crusade in Belfast for the very large supplies of the Gospels of John,

Scripture booklets and gospel leaflets. We thank you again for the four eighteen tonne containers of the literature which you have already sent this year, and I understand that you are now preparing a fifth container of literature for India. Please remember that all the literature which you send to us has a vital part in the evangelisation of the unreached multitudes of India.

Many church and mission leaders have been distributing these publications, and they write to tell us that these printed missionaries, with the blessing of the Lord, are very effective in winning souls to our Lord Jesus Christ.

The headquarters of our mission is in Madras from where the literature which you send to us is distributed all over this vast country. We are praying that our relationship with you will grow stronger, as together we witness for our Lord Jesus Christ to the millions of India.

From Dr. W. Scott and friends of India Bible Literature Mission.

Encouraged by these reports and letters from people all over India requesting instruction about the way of salvation or soliciting more literature, the Every Home Crusade stepped up its supply of the Gospel of John and Scripture booklets, leaflets and tracts to this densely populated country.

During a recent visit to Northern Ireland Dr. Scott shared the following testimony with the Every Home Crusade staff.

An evangelist in the city of Bangalore was using tracts that you print in the Every Home Crusade factory in Belfast.

He was giving those tracts out to people as they were passing in the street. A Sikh man came along and he took one of the tracts, walked some distance, read it and then he went on his way.

A week or so later that same evangelist was standing on the same street when the same Sikh man came, and he said, "You're the man that gave me that tract."

"Yes," replied the Evangelist.

The man went on, "Do you have anything else?"

The evangelist had other booklets which he gladly gave to the inquirer. The man then said, "Do you know what happened to me that day when I took this tract from you last week? I was walking to a railway track to commit suicide as I had planned. My life was totally devastated, I had no hope. You stopped me, you gave me that tract, I went on, stopped and I read it."

He read the tract that was produced on your machine and through his reading, standing there on a street in Bangalore that man became a new creature in Christ, he accepted Jesus Christ as his Saviour. He said, "My life was changed. I did not go and commit suicide. I went back to my home, and I was reconciled to my wife and family, and I am now back because I want to read more of God's Word."

Not only was one life saved, but his whole family came to Christ in an area where there wasn't a church. Now they have become a witnessing prayer group with other families who have accepted Jesus Christ to be their Saviour. Little is much when God is in it.

This close and fruitful co-operation between the India Bible Literature Mission and Every Home Crusade has grown and developed so much that during 1998 Every Home Crusade sent 150 tonnes of literature in eleven languages to Madras for distribution.

Substantial supplies of gospel literature are also sent to Mr. John Pandi of the Gospel Literature Outreach Ministries which is also located in Madras. Currently the Crusade sends an eighteen tonne container to India every four weeks.

Eastern Europe

In Eastern Europe the Crusade's literature has proved to be very fruitful as it has been used in evangelism. When the Iron Curtain fell with the collapse of communism in Russia in 1989, a great door opened to allow literature to freely enter the former Soviet Bloc countries. Tonnes of gospel literature were requested from various agencies in a diversity of languages, and Every Home Crusade lost no time in attending to these requests to help speed the gospel to lands that had formerly been closed.

There were two notable milestones in relation to the enterprise into Eastern Europe. When the doors opened to Romania after the fall of Ceausescu's regime that had oppressed the people for decades, many mission agencies took the opportunity to set up ministries inside the country. Foremost among these was Child Evangelism Fellowship.

Tom Somerville of CEF, who led the advance into Romania from Vienna, approached Every Home Crusade about using their literature when he was home for daughter Jane's wedding. Jane was being married to Derek French, Carol Adams' brother. A great day was had by all as they joined in the festivities with the young couple. Later that day Tom Somerville approached Samuel Adams and said, "I came from Austria to do two jobs. One was to give my daughter's hand in marriage. The other was to speak to you about printing young people's tracts in the Romanian language for use in Moldova and Romania."

The contact was made, and subsequently Tom and Samuel were able to work out the practical details. Every Home Crusade would print translated Child Evangelism material in two colours and ship it out to the team in Romania. Initially Tom asked that they supply 2, 000,000 of these tracts over a period of two years. The Crusade was also able to furnish them with 500,000 copies of the sixteen page Scripture booklet, "The Way of Salvation".

During the course of the next few summers CEF teams loaded their cars full of these gospel publications and visited village after village, distributing gospel literature where there had been no former Christian witness. The CEF tracts provided an address where inquirers could write to enroll in a Christian correspondence course. As a result of visiting all these villages with the gospel, over 31,000 children enrolled and are actively doing the correspondence course.

So successful was this venture that after two years CEF requested Every Home Crusade to print and send another 2,000,000 of the same tracts to Romania. Other missionaries with CEF in various Eastern European countries followed the same programme of gospel literature distribution amongst young people in the rural villages of these respective countries.

Another milestone in Every Home Crusade sending literature to Eastern Europe was when a Belfast man contacted the Crusade and shared his vision for Albania. Cecil Gaw holds a responsible job in Northern Ireland, but for some years he has been devoting his holiday time to take Christian literature into Albania. This was one of the most strictly closed and intolerant of all the European Communist Bloc States and the last to abandon Marxism.

Almost as soon as Albania opened its frontiers to admit foreigners, Cecil and some friends set up a fund to enable them to evangelise these needy people. Over a period of several years they took hundreds of thousands of tracts and gospel booklets from Every Home Crusade to Albania and freely distributed the gospel. The tracts also entered Serbia and spread the gospel message in printed form to the Albanian-speaking people who lived there.

Cecil and his friends went to the borders of Albania when the Kosovo crisis arose and met thousands of refugees who were fleeing from the war in Serbia. They took social aid to the needy and displaced people, and they also provided gospel booklets for this largely Muslim people so that they could read about the gospel of the Jesus Christ for the very first time. Since the doors opened to this land which was bereft of the gospel for many years, Cecil and his friends have taken in over 2, 000,000 Scripture booklets and gospel publications into Albania.

In 1991 The Friends of Friedensstimme Mission wrote and requested a supply of the booklet, "The Way of Salvation Through our Lord Jesus Christ" in Russian.

> Dear Brother Adams,
>
> Thank you for your letter. We are so thankful to you that you are going to send these Scripture booklets to the Pastors in Siberia and Russia. These pastors have been writing so often asking for supplies of such literature. We were praying to the Lord that such booklets would be sent to them, and you in the Every Home Crusade are the answer to our prayers.
>
> I know that the pastors will be careful in the distribution of the booklets. Each region has a leading pastor, and he will distribute the booklets to each church and to each evangelist. There are over 2,000 congregations in this part of Russia - small ones and larger ones. Each church would like to engage in evangelism and soul-winning, but they do not have the needed gospel literature. Your shipment of the booklets will be sent to the address in Novosibirsk and will be shared in areas like Yukot, Irkutsk, Kemerova, Abakan, etc.
>
> Some of the churches operate gospel literature vans, and they will be grateful if they can give these Scripture booklets to those who come to these vans. Our evangelists visit the prisons, and some of the prisoners plead for a gospel tract or booklet. During a prison visit with gospel literature, Gerhard Friessen wondered if he would get out alive. The prisoners pushed so hard to get even one gospel tract. You do not know how thankful we are that you are going to send us eighteen tonnes of these Russian Scripture booklets.
>
> From
>
> A. Pankratz, of Friedensstimme Mission

In answer to this request the Crusade prepared an eighteen tonne container of Scripture booklets and gospel tracts for Novosibirsk in Central Russia. A week before the container was due for shipment the Crusade's leadership learned that the Russian authorities would charge for a minimum of two containers no matter how small their shipment. They faced a dilemma for they did not have enough literature printed in the Russian language to take advantage of a second container. However, with the collapse of the notorious Iron Curtain, many aid agencies were transporting food and clothing to Eastern Bloc countries to help them through their severe winters. Ernie and Samuel called the Crusade staff together and explained to them their problem about sending an extra container, and suggested that they appeal to the churches and friends to fill the second container with warm clothing to send to the Russian Christians in Novosibirsk. A request was sent out to evangelical churches in East Belfast to participate in the project.

At first it seemed an impossible task to fill a twenty-foot-long container with clothing in five days, but during the course of the next week there was an endless stream of vehicles of all kinds arriving at Clara Street laden with clothing. Teams of ladies volunteered to pack the clothing into parcels and bags, as buses, vans, cars and trucks continued to drop off more donations of clothes. By the end of the week the second container was tightly packed with good clothes, and the Crusade's store was stacked high with enough clothing to fill another two containers. This surplus clothing was channelled to other evangelical agencies which specialised in sending relief to other worthy causes in these liberated lands.

The two containers were shipped to Russia at the same time, one containing warmth for the physical body and the other the Bread of Life for hungry souls.

The open door to Russia has not only resulted in an urgency to speed the message of the gospel to those who are hungry to hear about Jesus Christ, but also many church groups have sprung up all over the country. Many of these groups write to the Every Home Crusade to request tools of evangelism. Here is one such letter.

Dear Brother Adams,

Thank you for your prompt reply to our request. We are very grateful to hear such good news from you that you will supply us with large quantities of your Russian Scripture booklet "The Way of Salvation Through our Lord Jesus Christ" and also the children's Scripture tracts. We will be grateful to receive 500,000 of these booklets and of each of the children's tracts.

Our Union of Pentecostal churches of evangelical faith was formed in 1989. Our purpose of unification was to commence a wide evangelistic campaign throughout our country. There are now 230 churches in our Union in Belarus, and about fifteen churches have been formed in Central Russia and in Siberia. About forty-five new churches were formed during 1993. We have eight evangelistic teams in full-time ministry. All this sounds wonderful, but there is still a lot of opposition. We are looking for and waiting for a greater revival.

From Leonid Biriouk

The Crusade continues to receive many requests for evangelistic material in many languages from Eastern Europe and it is difficult to keep up with the demand. As I write, the Crusade is sending 150,000 Gospels of John booklets to the Ukraine and 400,000 gospel tracts are being prepared for Poland.

Africa

Jim Gillette is an American missionary who heads up the ministry of Ireland Outreach in Dalkey, which is located on the southern outskirts of Dublin. Part of Ireland Outreach's ministry is conducting the Emmaus Correspondence Bible Courses throughout Ireland and beyond. This ministry has opened many doors for the gospel which otherwise might have been difficult or even impossible to enter. Besides coordinating the courses from Dalkey, Mr. Gillette was invited to set up the same programme in Nigeria.

He visited West Africa and established the Emmaus Correspondence Course in Nigeria, and a good number of Christians completed the initial course. Many of these were invited to be official markers in strategic areas. To encourage these markers to recruit others for the correspondence courses Every Home Crusade was invited to provide a five kilo parcel of gospel literature for each marker to distribute within his own area.

One person the Lord provided for this programme was Dr. Ebenezer Obey who for over thirty years was one of Africa's most sought after super-star musicians with an outstanding record of over twenty gold and three platinum discs. Dr. Obey initially established a "Help Ministry", using his money to support the work of God in churches, in other ministries and to individuals. He also opened his doors to missionaries and ministers of God, both at home and from different parts of the world. When he finally abandoned his music career, Ebenezer Obey established a soul-winning ministry. He employed the services of a full-time pastor as minister-in-charge, with the pre-occupation of winning new converts and sending them to other churches for necessary follow-up and spiritual growth. He now directs the Ebenezer Obey Evangelistic Ministries (EOEM) which has the Decross Gospel Mission as its church-arm. This has now grown to a congregation of 2,500 people in less than three years. Apart from his church congregation, Evangelist Obey also reaches out to the masses either in the urban cities or in the rural areas of Nigeria through crusades and revival programmes.

Dr. Obey not only became involved with the Emmaus Correspondence Courses, but when he heard of Every Home Crusade and their literature ministry, he was keen to become involved with the Crusade.

Hundreds of Nigerian pastors faithfully write to the Crusade requesting evangelistic literature for their churches. However, delivery of these supplies created some problems with logistics. Postal services in Nigeria were not always reliable. Furthermore, it was expensive for Nigerians to correspond with the United Kingdom and Ireland. Dr. Obey helped out in this regard. He has a warehouse and the means to import a lot of literature. He corresponded with Samuel Adams and arranged for the five kilo parcels to be sent in a container. In Nigeria he set up a network whereby the parcels are dispatched and delivered to addresses within the country or to small depots at Christian bookshops in the main cities where the parcels will be collected. He also took the responsibility to provide an address in Nigeria to which Nigerians could write to the Crusade. Dr. Obey then sends this mail in bulk to the Clara Street offices in Belfast. This system is not only more efficient, but it also saves a lot of expense both for Every Home Crusade and for those who want to write to the Crusade.

This arrangement was so successful that a similar programme with the Emmaus Bible Correspondence Course and Every Home Crusade literature was set up in neighbouring Ghana under the leadership of Benjamin Boateng of Challenge Enterprises.

In 1996 Jim Mason, a missionary with SIM International, introduced a project to provide book sets of Bible study books for African pastors. Each set contained about twenty-five books consisting of Bible commentaries, sermon helps, Bible studies and pastoral procedures. In Nigeria alone 15,000 pastors benefited from this initiative. As part of the programme Jim approached Every Home Crusade and asked if they would supply sample packs of gospel tracts, leaflets and booklets for all these pastors. There was a lot of work involved in preparing 15,000 packets with sixty different items in each unit and sending them by container to Nigeria. Soon after their delivery, requests for gospel literature began to filter through from other pastors to use in their regions.

Latin America

At the same time Jim also introduced the programme for Christian workers in Chile, Paraguay, Uruguay, Bolivia and Peru. The Every Home Crusade sent another 10,000 sample packets of Spanish literature to pastors in these Latin American countries. Again this programme resulted in numerous requests for literature from the pastors who benefited from the "Books to Pastors" programme.

Brazil

For the last twenty years Brazil has enjoyed an extraordinary time of blessing and church growth. One of the characteristics of that church is their zeal for evangelism. Most churches are engaged in planting other churches, and it is hard to find a church that does not have at least one daughter congregation.

Every Home Crusade has printed millions of Scripture booklets and gospel tracts in the Portuguese language to help Brazilian Christians with their evangelistic drive. However, they encountered problems in sending the containers of literature to Brazil, because it was difficult to find people who would be responsible for the storage and distribution of such large quantities. Just then a missionary friend wrote to them.

> Dear brother Adams,
>
> Ademir Cardoso has a team of thirty full-time Christian workers who are witnessing for our Lord Jesus Christ in eight areas of the Amazon Basin. He is more than willing to handle your containers and has the necessary experience. He also has the means of delivering the literature to any part of Brazil.
>
> Gavin Aitken.

A letter was sent to establish contact with Ademir Cardoso, and he sent an encouraging reply to the Every Home Crusade.

> Dear Brother Adams,
>
> Your letter brought much joy to my heart. How good it is to know that there are people like you in the Every Home Crusade who are seeking to fulfil the Great Commission of our Lord Jesus Christ. For the past nine years I have been engaged in evangelising this country of Brazil from North to South distributing New Testaments, John's Gospels and other gospel literature. It hurts me that millions of persons

have not heard the gospel message. We really need your help with very large supplies of your publications.

Please send us one million copies of your Portuguese Scripture booklets, "The Way of Salvation Through Our Lord Jesus Christ" and "The Gospel of Jesus Christ, the Light of the World." Please also send us 200,000 copies of the Gospel of John in Portuguese and as many as you can send of the booklet, "Pardon and Assurance."

From Ademir Cardoso

The Crusade dispatched a container of Scripture booklets, tracts and the Gospel of John to Ademir, and a subsequent letter from Gavin Aitken indicated how the literature was being used.

Dear Brother Adams,

Ademir has put a parcel in the mail for you today with letters from and photos of two hundred young converts. They have been converted as the result of the Lord's blessing on the work of evangelism in the Amazon Basin. His whole idea in writing to you is to encourage you to be strong in this ministry of the printed page, because through it many souls are being won to our Lord Jesus Christ.

From Gavin Aitken

Ron Milligan has been a missionary in Brazil with the Pocket Testament League for more than thirty years. In their evangelistic crusades they have been using the Every Home Crusade literature. From Brazil Ron wrote to the Crusade:

Dear Brother Adams,

We are anxiously awaiting the arrival of another of your containers of literature in the Portuguese language. We held a wonderful gospel campaign in Minas Gerais, and thousands of copies of the Gospel of John were distributed. We held thirty-nine open-air meetings and showed gospel films forty-four times in nineteen towns and villages, over a fifty day period. Over 2,000 persons responded to the gospel invitation and are now enrolled in our Bible Study Course.

I have just received a letter from a man requesting some gospel booklets and Bible Study Lessons for relatives and friends. He obtained a copy of the Gospel of John in the City of Belo Horizonte and started to read it there and then. He told me how the Holy Spirit had enlightened his mind as he read the third chapter of John's Gospel. There on the street he accepted Jesus as his personal Saviour! He also sent a donation in support of our ministry.

Our stock of the Gospel of John is shrinking. Please print for us another 50,000 copies. We deeply appreciate your generosity in providing us with these gospels completely free of charge. I would say that our ministry would have been drastically curtailed if it had not been for the supply of these gospels which we received from you friends in the Every Home Crusade in Belfast.

From Missionary Ron Milligan,
The Pocket Testament League,
Brazil.

China

In April 1999 a friend of the ministry of the Every Home Crusade phoned the office and made an appointment to meet Ernie and Samuel. When he arrived he introduced the Crusade leaders to an Australian who uses the pseudonym "Brother Mak." Brother Mak is in his mid-thirties and has a very great burden for China. Samuel Adams said, "I have never met a man who had such evident burden for people and a commitment to work for their salvation."

Brother Mak produced a large map of China measuring eight feet by five feet. On it were pin pointed many of the cities he had been reaching with the gospel by means of literature. He explained that for four years he had studied and researched all about China. He had devised a plan whereby tourists from the United States, Europe and Australia, could distribute literature while visiting in inland China. What he needed was more literature in the Chinese language for this most densely populated country in the world.

Samuel said he had never met a person so well prepared. He had camera-ready copies of the leaflets he wanted printed plus a translation of all that was written on them. Each tract was complete, but it could be divided into three parts to make three separate tracts. On the tracts a contact address was provided as well as instructions of how to tune in to gospel radio broadcasts.

The Every Home Crusade accepted the challenge and printed several consignments, one being 600,000 of these gospel tracts. On 26th August 1999, these were dispatched to China via a third country. From there the tracts, like precious seed, are being sown all over China. Their work is daring and hazardous. Brother Mak wrote to the Crusade of the work that was being accomplished through the literature.

> Dear Samuel,
>
> During this month we have been distributing tracts in over 100 cities in China. Last week a team flew into China. One night at 11:00 p.m. everyone took to the streets to distribute the gospel tracts into the letter boxes of various homes. By 2:00 a.m. two sisters were caught by a plain clothed policeman and taken to the police station with your literature. By 2:30 p.m. the next day the ladies were released with cancelled visas (21 days to be out of the country). These sub-team members, after their first night out, were fired up more than ever and were determined to finish the job of evangelism which they came to do in China.
>
> We then took a bus to another city. I put together another itinerary, and they carried on the work with more zeal, wisdom and experience than before and finished their work. Glory! The Word of God is not bound, and the Word must

be preached as a witness to all, even the authorities. We have had a problem because we do not have enough of these tracts to give out. It tears our hearts out to be in the mountains, or the villages and run out of tracts to distribute. I am wanting to get a big surplus supply here in China. I can use one million tracts if you can send them to us. Thank you once again for printing the gospel message for China.

"Bro. Mak."

Cuba

For some years the Crusade endeavoured to send Christian literature to Cuba but with little success. The parcels were sent to individuals, and these were intercepted by the Communist authorities and confiscated. However, early in 1999 there was a change of heart. A missionary in Latin America made frequent visits to Cuba and through him we were able to establish a good contact.

In the March 1999 edition of the "Good News" news letter the following was reported.

For a few months we have heard reports that Scriptures have been imported into Cuba legally. We had been encouraged by a missionary society to try to ship 100,000 Gospels of John into Cuba with permission. At first little appeared to happen, then at the beginning of March we were asked for six sample copies of the "Gospel of John - Seven Steps to Knowing God". At the same time we were told that Cuban authorities like containers arriving to be completely full.

Because we can put about 400,000 Gospels of John into a container we applied for permission to ship this number. We have now received news from the organisation responsible for importing Scriptures. They are very

> grateful for your gift of 400,000 Gospels. They further stated, "However, we would like to receive one million copies of the Gospel of John so we can distribute some of these to other evangelical churches and then give the major quantity to the organisations to whom you specify."
>
> This is a wonderful opportunity to get God's Word into a country which has been closed to the gospel for so long.
>
> We have also been told that permission has been given for the football stadiums to be used in the month of June for gospel crusades. Please pray that many precious souls in Cuba will come to accept Jesus Christ to be their Saviour.

Two containers have already been transported to Cuba in 1999 carrying 720,000 Gospels of John. During the gospel crusades held on the island last summer the Every Home Crusade's publication of "John's Gospel- Seven Steps to Knowing God" were distributed, and many others were given to churches for their use. This is a great development considering that Cuba is still ruled by Communism. There has been little response to these consignments sent out from the Crusade as no international address is furnished on them.

Papua New Guinea

While the Crusade printed the gospel in seventy languages, they entered a new field in 1993 when they agreed to publish the portions of the New Testament which a missionary had translated for the very first time in the Ata language. Paul McIlwaine of New Tribes Mission works among the Ata tribe in Papau New Guinea. His primary work has been the painstaking work of the translation of the Scriptures into this tribal language. When he had reduced some of the Scriptures to the Ata language he contacted Every Home Crusade and gave them the privilege of printing the first Scriptures for the Ata people.

Paul's linguistic helper is a member of the tribe, and he wrote to Every Home Crusade from Papua New Guinea.

> My name is Kaikou. I am now a Bible Teacher, and I am involved in translating the New Testament into our Ata language. We live in very deep bush on top of mountain ranges and along rivers. Through hearing of the love of God and the gospel of our Lord Jesus Christ some of our people are Christians and are waiting for His return.
>
> Up until 1993 no one had translated God's Word into our language. Today we constantly praise God for the Scripture booklets printed in Belfast, so that His talk which was hidden has now been revealed to us. We now have portions of God's Word in our hands. We also now have schools where our people teach others to read our language. Our people are now able to read the Bible, and it is clear to them.
>
> God's work is going ahead in our midst too. He has raised up over fifty Bible teachers and trainees who are teaching His Word in ten different churches of His people. The Christians in these churches usually meet three times each week for teaching, singing and praying. They also remember our Lord's sacrifice in the way He taught us so to do. We are hoping to finish the work of translation of the New Testament by the end of this year, 1998. (sic)

Ethiopia

During the last two decades Ethiopia hit the headlines around the world for all the wrong reasons. Devastating famine, cruel war and extreme poverty was what was envisaged in people's minds. The problems have not been solved, but behind the bad headlines of the secular press a great spiritual harvest is being reaped, and the printed page is contributing greatly to this blessing. Gerald Gotzen gave the Every Home Crusade staff an account of the work of printed missionaries in that country in September, 1999.

The only way I can describe what is happening in Ethiopia is an "explosion of the Gospel." I have travelled around Europe, Asia, practically all the countries of Africa and sometimes to America, but I have never witnessed myself such a response to the Lord Jesus Christ. Now is the time for the distribution of the Word of God and literature. There is a need; there is a demand; there is an urgency, and people want to read.

Ethiopia is not like our Western countries where although people can produce very good literature some people will read it, and some people will immediately bin it, but out there practically any type of literature whether it's colourful, well produced or simply produced, people will read it.

In Ethiopia not everyone is literate - you will see children reading either the Bible or some Gospel literature to their parents. The children have to read slowly and carefully. Sometimes they will have to repeat a verse or sentence that perhaps the parents didn't understand the first time. I have seen this in villages in the mountains without electricity, and it's either by a smelly oil lamp or a flickering candle, and in this way so many people are coming to Christ.

We want to thank you for the container of literature you sent us. In your container we received 2,000,000 copies of "The Way of Salvation" in Amharic. These booklets have been distributed in Ethiopia North, West, South and East. They've been very much used in evangelistic outreach campaigns, whether in villages or towns or in cities. They are literally being used in the highways and the byways.

Because Ethiopia is very mountainous there are so many valleys and rivers where not even a Land Rover can cross them at times. In such cases we use mules for transportation of the evangelists, and we use mules for the transportation of the Bibles and the literature. We actually bought four gospel mules. These mules are very sturdy and very stubborn, but they've really got stamina, and they're bringing the Word of God and this Gospel literature right into the remote regions.

Your Scripture booklets are penetrating both the Orthodox and the Moslem population. Ethiopia is about thirty-five percent Moslem. Some of these are moderate and some are fanatical, but because "The Way of Salvation" booklets are just Scripture, many Moslems will accept them. I don't know any other country in the world where there are so many Moslems turning to the Lord. I know of at least three small villages where once a mosque dominated the village and five times a day the people would pray to Allah. Now, through the power of God, the mosque building is still there, but the sign of the crescent has now been replaced by the sign of the cross, and they are calling on the name of Jesus.

Last week I visited the office of a Gospel Printing Press in Ethiopia. Sitting at the table opposite me was a man named Alabi, who had been a Moslem up to the age of thirty, he's now about thirty-six. He has a doctorate in the Koran - he knew the Koran by heart, and the Koran is about one-third the size of the Bible. He studied seven years in Iran, and then he was appointed to a high position in another Moslem country. He was a devoutly religious Moslem who unfailingly prayed five times a day.

Before a Moslem actually prays, he must bathe so that he is absolutely clean. One day when Alabi was about to wash he heard a voice, whether it was audible or in his heart it's difficult to say, but he said it was real to him. The voice spoke in his language and said to him, "Alabi, why are you going through this ritual every day. If you trust Me you can be cleansed and set free for ever?"

He said that the voice was so real he turned round as if somebody was speaking to him, and then he began to look around and say "Who are you?" There was no reply.

The next day was Friday, so he went into the principal mosque in the capital. While he was at the service in the mosque, there was an evangelist called Daniel who was praying in his home. He felt from the Lord that he ought to go and stand in front of the mosque. This mosque is massive, thousands go to it, but as they were all leaving after the service, Daniel went up to Alabi and said, "I believe I'm here to speak to you."

"I believe you are," said Alabi. They both went back to Daniel's house where Daniel spoke to him from the Scriptures, and Alabi gave his life to the Lord Jesus Christ. Since then Alabi has had to leave his native country and come to live in Ethiopia, where he has since led seventy other Moslems to faith in Christ.

Appeals

Much of the correspondence which arrives at the Crusade office requests for literature in different language groups. It is a step of faith for the Crusade to be able to attend to these requests. This is typical of many letters which arrive at the Crusade's office.

Dear Brother Adams,

It is very encouraging for us to know that we can obtain a twenty-foot container of literature for free distribution. We can use this material here in Panama, and we can send part of it over land to Nicaragua. We can also use some literature in French, which we can send from here to Haiti.

With this in mind, the quantities we are thinking of are:

In Spanish for Panama & Nicaragua:

200,000 "Gospel of John"; 170,000 "Gospel of Jesus Christ" Scripture booklet; 170,000 "The Way of Salvation" - Scripture booklet; one million assorted gospel tracts in twelve titles; and 90,000 "Pardon and Assurance" booklets.

In French for Haiti:

30,000 "Gospels of John"; 15,000 "Gospel of Jesus Christ" - Scripture booklet; 15,000 "The Way of Salvation" booklets; and 10,000 "Pardon and Assurance" booklets.

We wish you God's richest blessings.

Gerardo Scalante

An eighteen tonne container was sent to Gerardo with literature for these Central American language groups.

Gospel literature from Every Home Crusade is reaping a great harvest of souls for Christ every day in many parts of the world. Distribution depots have been established in strategic cities in Africa, Asia and South America, and from there the Word of God is sent to other cities, towns, hamlets and individuals.

When sufficient requests from one country justify sending an eighteen tonne container shipment to a distributor, the Crusade is always ready to do this providing the distributor is able to make adequate arrangements to receive such a load. Where it is necessary, the Crusade will send a gift to the receiving party to either pay, or help pay for any customs clearance costs or internal transport in the receiving country.

Publishing the gospel of Jesus Christ is Every Home Crusade's method of fulfilling the Great Commission in which Jesus Christ commanded His church to take the gospel into all the world. It is the joy and delight of those who have the privilege to be involved in doing so. The results like the profits, are eternal.

Truly the promise given to Ernie Allen back in 1936 has been realised, "If you give your life to Me, I will give you a life of blessing." The work of Every Home Crusade grew out of that one dedicated life. Ernie Allen and his friends have been sowing on earth in order to reap a great harvest in heaven.

Chapter Sixteen

I Am Surprised

For years plywood tea chests have transported Britain's favourite beverage from India and Africa to our shores. Every Home Crusade returned the compliment and sent the same tea chests back to India and Africa plus scores of other countries, filled with literature which spoke of the Living Water which is able to satisfy people so that they need never thirst again.

The quantities of literature being sent out became so great at the end of 1992 that it was necessary to use eighteen tonne containers to transport the precious cargo of the gospel literature to Africa, Asia, Central and South America. Very soon containers would also be used to carry the same literature to the newly liberated countries of Eastern Europe after their long enslavement under Communist regimes. Tea chests were later replaced with cardboard boxes previously used for tea or videos to neatly pack the literature.

Year after year the production at the Gospel Literature Factory increased by twenty percent annually. This meant increased costs for paper, extra machinery and transportation. The income of the

Crusade more than doubled between 1992 and 1998 allowing them to keep pace with demands and requests. Some older presses were sold, and the money made was used towards the purchase of new equipment. Some legacies enabled the Crusade to make the improvements that were needed. Another Sormz press was purchased. Notice of this was published in the "Good News" publication of August 1993.

> Due to the increasing demand for the literature we are selling two of our smaller printing machines and are buying a large Heidelberg Sormz printing machine which will increase our output. This exchange will cost us £11,000. At this time we are also needing a new large collator for the production of large numbers of booklets. This will cost about £25,000. Please pray for the Lord's provision for the increasing financial needs of the work.

The Lord met the need for a new collator also, and the production of literature continued to grow.

With the passing of time the introduction of new machines soon began to crowd the new premises at Clara Street. It became impossible to convene conferences in the factory as the machines were too heavy to be relocated for one day. The increased demand also meant that the quantity of paper for one month and the boxes of printed literature were too much to be stored in the allocated area.

One evening a group of Christians came to see the factory in operation. Presses rolled out the literature, the collator fitted the booklets in order, the stitcher performed well and the folding went very smoothly. After the demonstration the visiting group had a committee meeting to which they invited Samuel. Late that night while the committee meeting continued Samuel withdrew from the meeting and spoke to a friend who was present with the visiting group. Samuel explained that the rapid growth of their work meant that the factory was already too confined for the equipment and machines, and he had thought of adding a mezzanine floor above the print shop as a store. He wanted the minimum number of supporting peers on the factory floor. This would free up some needed space for storage. For fifteen minutes the friend looked around the print shop and then said to Samuel, "Leave it with me, and I will do it for you."

Samuel understood this to mean that he would supply the steel supports. However, on the morning the workmen arrived, they were accompanied by joiners. The friend did the whole job as a free gift to the Crusade. This extension gave them relief for the storage of lighter items, but they still needed a store for the tonnes of paper that arrived each month.

In June 1997 edition of "Good News" another notice appeared.

> We have never been so busy as we are now trying to supply millions of our publications in answer to the urgent appeals from many parts of the world. We are sure that the Lord is leading us to go forward in a great advance of the work.
>
> A large Heidelberg Speedmaster 72 ZP printing machine has now been ordered. We have also arranged to take over a large paper store which is convenient to our factory. By using this store we will have room for the new printing machine. We will also need to have a fork-lift in the new store, and a lorry will be needed to transport the paper to the factory.

This expansion was partly due to the printing of the Gospels of John in many languages, and these were in great demand all over the world. They acquired a 4,000 square foot store to rent in a former mill just a mile away from the factory on the Beersbridge Road. They purchased a truck and another fork-lift for use in the store. This new accommodation meant they could order 200 tonnes of paper at one time and still have room to store the printed material before shipping it out in containers.

This move gave more room for the imminent increase in production. Ernie and Samuel were advised that another large printer with a folding machine and a saddle stitcher would allow them to produce two Gospels of John in one process. There was much discussion and consideration about the expense of this. Again the Lord supplied the resources to make these purchases in a remarkable way.

Just at that time a lady supporter in Co. Tyrone died and left her house to the Crusade for the furtherance of the gospel. This seemed to be a green light signal for Ernie and Samuel to proceed with the purchases.

Offers of reconditioned presses began to arrive from England and Europe. No move was made as Samuel felt there could be something better available. Within a short time a friend in the printing trade made Samuel and Ernie aware that the exact machine they were looking for was available at a very good price, but they would have to move quickly.

On the way home from the office Samuel prayed for guidance. He reckoned that other equipment would also be needed and this would bring the expenditure to more than £240,000. Samuel felt that if there was one more substantial gift given to the Crusade it would encourage them to take the step and buy the machine.

When he arrived home in Drumbo, Samuel received a phone call from a man who inquired about the Crusade. The caller said he would like them to meet that night. At that encounter the friend gave him an envelope which contained the confirmation Samuel had prayed for - a gift of £5,000 for the work.

The next day Samuel and Clive went to see the machine of which they had been told. It was exactly what they wanted. After some negotiation they settled on purchasing the machine for £71,000. Another £10,000 was spent on upgrading the printing press. When news of this deal reached the agent in England he was astounded that they were able to buy a Heidelberg 102 ZP for this price.

The purchase of machines and paper are often a testimony to unbelievers in the printing trade. Many of them just cannot believe that this factory runs on faith and that they do not print to make money. One of the agents who sold them sixty tonnes of paper in 1998, often brings agents from his company in England to see the factory and has Samuel or Ernie explain the operation to them. The visitors leave the factory astounded at what goes on in this most unusual factory.

When the saddle stitcher was purchased, the Crusade was able to sell the Duplo collating machine which was made redundant with the arrival of the new equipment. The agent and owner of the company where they bought the stitcher was not a believer. He initially offered them £15,000 for their old machines. The following week he called and said he would pay the Crusade £20,000 for he was amazed at how the funds were raised for the Crusade work. He told Samuel that he would make his profit elsewhere.

With this new press plus the saddle stitcher and folder, they had the capacity to print and produce 50,000 Gospels of John in one day. These gospels carry an attractive coloured cover which is also printed on the presses. These machines are supervised by a team of three young men who joined the Crusade in recent years.

Gary Bolton from Belfast who had a remarkable conversion to Jesus Christ, got involved in the work of the Every Home Crusade after he visited the factory to pick up a supply of tracts to be used in an evangelistic programme in Dublin. He works in the stitching and folding process with Gary Boal from Culcavey.

Gary Boal had shown interest in entering into full-time Christian work for over a year. As he prayed about this step a vacancy arose at the Every Home Crusade, and the young man felt this was God's opening for him.

The third member of this operational team is Philip Hunter. Philip works four days a week at the factory, and he is also in training to become a pastor of an Elim Church. He had already gained some experience as the assistant pastor at Crumlin Elim Church.

Simon Wade from Drumbo plays a part by fitting in to help wherever he is needed on the factory floor. After he left school he worked on a temporary basis at the Crusade. During this time the young man felt Lord was speaking to him and encouraging him to surrender his life to the Lord and His guidance.

Samuel Adams is responsible for the impressive and colourful art work on the covers of the various booklets which has greatly enhanced the appearance and quality of the literature.

In December 1998 the "Good News" monthly report gave details of publishing for 1998:

> Dear friend, join with us in praising the Lord for His blessing upon this ministry during the past year and for the tremendous privilege of serving His Church in over 100 countries of the world by freely sending out millions of copies of the Gospel of John and other Scripture and gospel publications in about seventy different languages.
>
> Our printing record for this year is as follows:
>
> 27,523,000 Gospels of John, Scripture Booklets, Gospel and Revival Booklets
>
> 16,848,000 Gospel Tracts and Revival Leaflets
>
> The Total Number of Publications was 44,371,000.
>
> Over sixty tonnes of the literature were sent out during this month of December alone. These included eighteen tonnes to India and another eighteen tonne container of the literature sent to Kenya. In these containers there were millions of the Gospel of John, Scripture Booklets, and other gospel leaflets and gospel tracts.
>
> During the month we also sent 50,000 Gospels of John to Russia for Friedensstimme Mission. 50,000 Gospels of John in the Spanish language were sent to Spain for distribution to pastors and for evangelistic work in schools and hospitals.
>
> It is expected that by the end of this year over 750 tonnes of literature will have left the factory for the needy mission fields of the world. Samuel Adams insists, "We could not produce this volume of output of gospel literature without

the dedicated work of the whole staff. At Clara Street the nineteen full-time staff members and six voluntary workers who come for at least one day a week, pull their weight as a team to make sure that the gospel is sent from the Gospel Literature Factory to the millions in over 100 countries.

Fred Orr has worked in Brazil for more than forty-five years, and he wrote to them in appreciation of the Crusade's work.

Dear friends of the Every Home Crusade,

I want to thank you on behalf of the Acre Gospel Mission for all the literature which you have sent to us in Brazil. Let me tell you of how the Lord uses your gospel literature. After one of our meetings a man said to me, "You know, we are not immortal. Tonight I am going to make the decision of my life." He said to me, "Your young Christians for over a year, have been putting gospel literature into my home, and I have been reading pages from the Bible. Jesus is the only Way. He paid a debt that He did not owe."

I asked him, "Who owed it?"

He replied, "I did. You did, and He paid our debt."

That evening I led that man to the Saviour. I heard him praying, "Save me O God, in the name of Jesus, Save me."

Beloved, the Lord has promised that His Word shall not return unto Him void.

Fred Orr

Amazonas, Brazil.

Chapter Seventeen

Surprised At The Blessings

Over a hundred years ago a convention met in United States to discuss, "How to Reach the Masses." During that week of convention meetings, a young man stood on a box at a street corner and began to preach. A crowd of working men gathered on their way home from work. They were so deeply moved by the sermon they forgot they were tired and hungry.

The crowd became so dense that they had to move. The preacher announced that he would preach again at the Academy of Music. They followed him down the street, and they filled the main floor of the building sitting with their lunch boxes under their arms, while he preached again with such power that they were moved to tears. The preacher had only a few minutes to preach because the convention on "How to Reach the Masses" was gathering in the same auditorium. While the convention was discussing how to reach the masses, D. L. Moody was doing it. He was preaching the kingdom of God, and many were pressing into it.

General Booth prayed, "Lord close up hell for one year and help us win the lost." To close hell is not possible, but reaching the lost is a divine compulsion and heart constraint that Ernie Allen has felt since he was a young man. It was that zeal and vision that led him to begin the Revival Movement out of which grew the Every Home Crusade. True revival is a practical matter. While others talked about revival, Ernie Allen did something about it. While revival is for the glory of God and the edifying of the church, it should result in salvation of the lost. Revival is God moving through His children with mighty power to accomplish His purpose.

The Every Home Crusade has been experiencing an unheralded revival for decades. Who can ever measure the impact that their tracts, leaflets, posters and booklets have made on lives in many lands and cultures? Tens of thousands of people have responded by letters to register their conversion to Jesus Christ.

The Gospel Literature Factory is a virtual hive of productive activity. Every worker is a testimony to the grace of God in individual lives. The leadership recognises the gracious hand of God guiding them during fifty years of constant growth. Every piece of machinery is a witness to the faithfulness of God who supplied the wherewithal to purchase it. Each piece of literature is sent out as a missionary and is soaked in earnest prayer so that it might touch and transform lives from the power of darkness and bring them into the Kingdom of God's dear Son. This building is not only used to publish the message of the gospel in multiple languages to multiplied millions, but the very building publicises how great God is.

At the present production level the factory uses three tonnes of paper each day on six printing presses. One tonne of paper can produce 640,000 gospel tracts or 106,000 "Power" leaflets or 80,000 Scripture booklets or 20,000 Gospels of John. These booklets have been the instruments God has used to bring eternal life to souls from all nations.

When W. J. Patton of Dromara wrote a book entitled, "Pardon and Assurance" he could never have envisaged that out of that book would come the booklet, "Pardon for Sin and Assurance of Peace with God." Ernie was very struck with the contents and simplicity of this book and spent days gleaning through it to put together this booklet. Millions of these have been printed in many languages. Mr. Patton's ministry lives on long after his earthly life finished, and through his printed messages thousands of people have been led to faith in the Lord Jesus Christ.

One of the most productive and fruitful programmes of the Every Home Crusade has been the use of the writings of Dr. J. C. Ryle, the former Anglican Bishop of Liverpool. Dr. Ryle was one of the foremost bishops of the Church of England during the eighteenth century. As well as his faithful and fruitful preaching, Dr. Ryle was a prolific author. He wrote many books on evangelistic themes, practical Christian living, historical biographies of the great English Reformers and commentaries on the Scriptures. Most of these publications became classics and best sellers. In 1849 he compiled a hymn book which bore the title Spiritual Songs.

It is not so well known that the godly bishop produced a series of gospel tracts which made him known far and near. As a young curate he zealously distributed tracts in Southampton. At that time he used the leaflets of the Religious Tract Society. In 1845 he produced a tract based on a sermon he had preached on Luke 7:40, "I have somewhat to say unto thee." He distributed the tract everywhere he went and tried to enthuse others to do the same. Following that he wrote almost 300 tracts which sold at one penny each and were widely circulated in the British Isles and throughout the British Empire. All of his tracts bore simple but pointed titles; Jesus the Saviour; Christ's Invitation; The Value of Your Soul; Hell; Temporal and Eternal; The Best Friend; How to Find happiness; How to Find Peace - these are only a few of his many tracts.

William Hunt of Ipswich published Dr. Ryle's tracts in seven small volumes with the title, "Home Truths." It is believed that about 12,000,000 of these tracts were distributed during Dr. Ryle's lifetime. They were translated into more than a dozen languages. Ryle was justly designated "the prince of tract writers."

Ryle's tracts have been used by many tract societies across the world. It is difficult if not impossible to improve on them. Early in Ernie Allen's ministry he began to print copies of Dr. Ryle's tracts and circulate them, first in Britain and then all over the world in different languages. It is estimated the presses of the Every Home Crusade have published more than 100,000,000 of Dr. Ryle's tracts.

Although the godly and zealous bishop has been with the Lord since 1916 his tract ministry still reaps a great harvest of precious souls through the agency of Every Home Crusade. Sometimes letters arrive at the Crusade from people in distant lands asking Ernie to give their greetings to Dr. J. C. Ryle and the Ulster Evangelist, W. P. Nicholson. That day will have to wait.

It certainly was more than a brainstorm when Ernie Allen had the vision to compile the Scripture booklets, "The Way of Salvation Through Our Lord Jesus Christ" and "The Gospel of Jesus Christ, the Light of the World." These booklets have put the Scriptures into the hands of millions of people in seventy different languages. More than 100,000,000 of these booklets in many languages have been shipped to over 100 countries, and almost every day letters arrive reporting conversions as a result of reading these booklets. Besides the correspondence that arrives in Belfast, many other distribution centres around the world process their own mail in the country where they work.

"The Gospel of John - Seven Steps to Knowing God," is a booklet that has been changing lives for many years. In the first nine months of 1999 alone, over 6,750,000 copies of these booklets were sent out by the Every Home Crusade.

The extraordinary Irish Evangelist, W. P. Nicholson, was greatly used of God in Ulster seventy years ago. Today his tracts are still touching many lives. Dr. Rueben Torrey, the American evangelist under whose ministry Ernie's mother was led to faith in Jesus Christ, still reaches men and women through the printed page. The Revival series booklets which Ernie Allen first published in 1948 are still produced, and millions of these have circulated around the globe for fifty years stirring up interest in revival in many hearts.

The ministry of Every Home Crusade is much like an iceberg, the greater part of which is hidden beneath the surface of the icy seas. The visitor to the Gospel Literature Factory in East Belfast can see the machines in operation and meet the workers, but the greater effect of what is seen in Clara Street is largely veiled from the human eye. The accomplishment of fifty years of faithful ministry can only be measured in eternity.

On Mother's Day, Sunday 14th March 1999, Ernie was preaching at a Morning Service in Tobermore, County Londonderry having already completed an earlier church service nearby in Draperstown; during the singing of the closing hymn Ernie felt a sudden weakness come over him. He sank into the pulpit seat while members of the congregation went to his aid. One lady in the congregation that morning, not a regular worshipper at that church, was a cardiac nurse and was able to care for Ernie until the arrival of the ambulance. Dazed and not sure what was happening, Ernie was rushed to the Mid-Ulster Hospital where it was discovered he had suffered what was described as a "silent heart attack" - a cardiac attack without any pain.

Mr. & Mrs. James Ballentine who were scheduled to provide hospitality for Ernie that day, took care of his personal effects and car. They contacted his wife and family who rushed to Ernie's bedside in the intensive care unit at the hospital in Magherafelt. They were informed that the next forty-eight hours would be critical for Ernie.

Although only family members were allowed to visit him, Samuel Adams was admitted to the Intensive Care Unit to be present with his close colleague. Although Ernie was ordered to strict rest he kept inquiring about the literature factory and encouraged Samuel to make sure the monthly report got out in time.

The opening paragraph of the March edition of the "Good News" reported the incident.

> We are very sorry to inform you that on Sunday the 14th March Mr. Allen had a heart attack. He is making slow but

> steady improvement day by day. The family and staff would appreciate your continued prayers for him. We would also like to thank many friends who have been praying for him at this time. On the 22nd of March we received a fax from Mr. E. Velayutham of the India Bible Literature Mission, who wrote, "We are very sorry to hear about Mr. Allen's heart condition. Tomorrow the staff of the India Bible Literature Mission will have a chain prayer meeting for his complete healing throughout the whole day. We praise God for your partnership with us and may God bless your ministry in a mighty way."

Many others from countries all over the world joined in prayer for God's servant. He benefited from the excellent nursing care at the hospital during the two weeks he was there. He was a bit frustrated when he was told that he would not be allowed to drive his car for some time. Scores of get-well cards flooded into his hospital ward, and various pastors endeavoured to visit him even though visiting was strictly controlled. God answered those many prayers, and Ernie Allen made a good and steady recovery. Perhaps it is more telling that through all his days of illness, he never lost his vision for the work, and his burden even augmented to send out greater quantities of literature than ever before.

Gradually he began to return to the factory, at first for one hour a day and then a little more each week, until he was back at his desk every day.

Ernie continues to enjoy opening the mail and reading what God is doing all over the world. He still is amazed at the tonnage of gospel literature that is shipped from the Gospel Literature Factory every year and is very happy still to have a hand on the helm of this great work.

On Friday morning, 17th July 1936, the Lord gave Ernie that promise, "If you give your life to me I will give you a life of blessing." God has not only fulfilled that promise, but the answer has been far beyond Ernie's wildest dreams.

The Lord gave Ernie a wife who has stood shoulder to shoulder with him in his life of faith and vision for the lost. Together Ernie and Kathleen were greatly blessed when their three children came to know the Lord Jesus Christ as Saviour and were never more delighted than when they also entered the ministry of the Every Home Crusade.

The Lord has also blessed Ernie with a great team of workers who are committed to his vision for the world. Samuel and Carol Adams were a wonderful gift from the Lord to the work of the Every Home Crusade. Supporters also have shown their confidence by their prayerful and financial backing for the work. The Lord gave Ernie a parish that reaches to the end of the earth, and He has greatly blessed this one life. No one is more surprised than Ernie Allen himself.

Every one who visits the Clara Street factory is surprised to see the sheer magnitude of the work. They are surprised at the modern machinery they see and the financial expenditure which in 1998 totalled almost £845,000 enabling them to send over 500 tonnes of literature all over the world. To operate and maintain the ministry of the Every Home Crusade it takes £2,300 per day, seven days a week for fifty-two weeks each year. They work without profits on their product and without guaranteed income, yet every day is a miracle at the gospel Literature Factory in Clara Street as God provides for their every need.

Ernie is grateful for the team of workers the Lord has given him. This quiet and mild mannered man who seldom raises his voice to a shout when preaching, has been a mighty instrument in the hand of his Lord. People are surprised at the modesty of Ernie Allen and all are overwhelmed at the effect this ministry is having around the world.

The story of Ernie Allen and the Every Home Crusade reminds me that God is Almighty and is full of surprises. Not that He is ever taken by surprise, but we are frequently surprised at Him. He feels no frustration, faces no barriers and entertains no fears. He is omnipotent, but we are weak. He is infinite, but we are finite. When we try to gauge God by our earthly and limited reason, then we are in for surprises.

Philip and Andrew, the disciples of our Lord Jesus Christ, employed earthly reason to gauge how to feed a multitude with insufficient resources. They got a surprise when the Lord fed 5,000 people with a boy's lunch which consisted of five loaves and two fishes. I am sure the boy who gave the lunch was surprised. However, I like to think that the boy's mother got the biggest surprise of all when her son arrived home and told her how the bread and fish she had prepared were used by the Lord Jesus to feed a great multitude.

As a young man Ernie Allen gave his all to the same Lord Jesus, and with what he gave, the Lord has fed even greater multitudes. I like to think of the surprise Ernie's mother will have when Ernie arrives home in heaven and tells her of the millions that were fed with the Bread of Life because of what she prepared in their simple home in Annahilt.

Are you surprised at this story? Give your all to the Lord Jesus, and He will give you a life of blessing. It will surprise you what God can do.

Invitation

As the work of Every Home Crusade continues to grow we need many more friends to pray and support this ministry of Printing the Gospel Message and sending it for distribution to many countries.

At this time we have in our office over 500 letters from around the world from National Pastors and Evangelists all requesting supplies of our Scripture and Gospel publications. We are in a very solemn position of responsibility as thousands of Pastors and Evangelists are looking to us for regular supplies of the literature, which are sent to them completely free of charge.

We would appeal to you for your prayers and support in this Mission to Millions of souls.

MY RESPONSE

With our Lord's help I will pray daily for the worldwide extension of the work of Every Home Crusade and Revival Movement Association and for much fruit that will remain for our Lord Jesus Christ. Please send me the monthly GOOD NEWS report of the work.
I have enclosed a gift of £ .... to help place the Gospel of John, the Scripture booklets and Gospel literature in the millions of empty hands in over 100 countries of the world.

NAME ....

ADDRESS ....

....

.... Postcode ....

Please write to: Mr. W. E. Allen, Every Home Crusade, 43 Oakland Avenue, Belfast, BT4 3BW, Northern Ireland

Note: If you wish to arrange for a group of friends to visit the factory in Clara Street, Belfast please telephone (028) 90 455026